Light Sitting in Light

A CHRISTIAN'S EXPERIENCE IN ZEN

Elaine MacInnes

Foreword by Shirley du Boulay

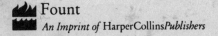

Fount

An Imprint of HarperCollins*Publishers*

DEDICATION

*In gratitude to all my teachers in both
Christianity and Buddhism.*

*Particularly to the memory of the
late Yamada Koun Roshi and the late
Rev. Hugo M. Enomiya-Lassalle SJ*

Fount Paperbacks is an Imprint of
HarperCollins*Religious*
Part of HarperCollins*Publishers*
77–85 Fulham Palace Road, London W6 8JB

First published in Great Britain
in 1996 by Fount Paperbacks

1   3   5   7   9   10   8   6   4   2

A catalogue record for this book is
available from the British Library

ISBN 0 00 627948 1

Printed and bound in Great Britain by
Caledonian International Book Manufacturer, Glasgow

Contents

Foreword

I had never met a Zen master before and I seem to remember expecting someone inscrutably Oriental, rather remote and forbidding, and most certainly male. Sister Elaine MacInnes is none of these things. Now in her early seventies, strongly built and white haired, she is direct, warm and friendly, her accent, despite over thirty years in the Far East, unmistakably Canadian. She has a serene and kindly air, great vitality, and eyes that see through you and beyond – an irresistible combination of wisdom and humour. She deserves that high tribute paid to St Teresa of Avila – she is 'extraordinarily ordinary'.

As one of the disciples authenticated by the famous Zen master Yamada Koun Roshi, Sister Elaine is one of a very small number of accredited Zen teachers in the world today and anyone taught by her can be confident that they are following the true tradition of Zen. In 1980, after nearly twenty years' arduous training, she and the German Jesuit priest Father Enomiya-Lassalle were the first Roman Catholics to be invested as *roshi* (the word literally means 'old teacher'), so she is one of the few Zen teachers who is also a member of a Roman Catholic religious order, in her case Our Lady's Missionaries, a Canadian missionary community founded in 1949.

Does she find it hard, being fully a Christian nun and teaching Zen? Far from it, she is at home with both, rejoices in both, finds that one complements and enriches the other. Through Western Christianity she finds the God of relationship, the 'I and Thou' of Martin Buber; through Eastern Spirituality she finds union with the God beyond all religions, where all creation is one. She is at home with the Christian mystics like Meister Eckhart, St John of the Cross, Jan van Ruysbroeck and Johann Tauler, who said: 'Diligent practice in the end demands that one should sink into the deepest ground. In those depths become that nothingness.' She does not attempt to Christianize Zen, she does not need to; for her it is all one.

The only concession she makes to Christianity in the *zendo*, the weekly meeting when meditation or 'sitting' is practised, is to place a cross surrounded by a circle (the Eastern symbol of formless perfection) next to the flowers, the incense sticks and the single candle. And sometimes she will allow herself to draw a parallel between Zen and Christianity, for instance saying how practising Zen helped her to reach a new and deeper understanding of St Paul's line 'I live, yet not I but Christ lives in me.' But people of all religions and of none come to her *zendo* and she prefers to let them discover any connections for themselves. For instance one memorable December evening we celebrated the night of the Buddha's enlightenment, most quietly and beautifully. At the end, still sitting on our cushions, we all slowly, and in deep silence, ate a tangerine and drank a cup of green tea. It was a profound experience and afterwards I said to Sister Elaine, 'That gives a whole new dimension to the Eucharist, doesn't it?' 'I didn't say so,' she replied, the pleasure in her eyes belying the firmness of her tone.

Zen is tough and in the *zendo* one sees another side of Sister Elaine, the strict disciplinarian. Shoes must be left outside the door, the cushions correctly aligned, the bells rung at precisely the right moment, the hardest of all for those with weak backs or stiff legs, absolute stillness must be maintained. The Zen masters used to say that you should sit like a mountain, for when the body is unmoving then it is easier for the mind to be quiet. There is no doubting the truth of this ideal and the peace of the *zendo* is an experience in itself – somehow even late arrivals or children playing in the street do not disturb it. Practitioners sit in lines facing the wall, while the teacher takes a central position, with a clear view of everyone in the room. Just when you long to wriggle you are most aware of her gimlet eyes boring into your back, daring you to give in. Resentment gives way to gratitude as you resist temptation and sink deeper into the quiet, remembering that she has experienced a far tougher regime, when, during her first months in Japan, she used to start at 3 o'clock in the morning and continue a pattern of sitting, (Zen prefers the word 'sitting' to 'meditating') working and very occasionally eating, until midnight – only sleeping for three hours a night.

Apart from the hour and a half of sitting, there are two other elements in the weekly *zendo*: *teisho* and *dokusan*. The nearest Western equivalent to the *teisho* would I suppose be the sermon, but in Sister Elaine's hands it is not something you would consider sleeping through. As she reads the *koans*, (conundrums beyond reach of the intellect) together with commentaries from the Zen masters, she catches each sitter's eye in turn, reading with an animation and confidence that makes one wonder if she could not have been an actress if she had so chosen. Imagine her spirited rendering of this *koan*:

> The wind was flapping the temple flag, and two monks were having an argument about it. One said, 'The flag is moving.' The other said, 'The wind is moving.' They argued back and forth but could not reach the truth. The sixth patriarch said, 'It is not the wind that moves. It is not the flag that moves. It is your mind that moves.' The two monks were struck with awe.

Tantalizing though these *koans* are, frustrated though we feel at not fully understanding them, her reading never fails to keep one's attention and subtly to urge one to continue sitting and to hope for greater insight; perhaps even, one day, to experience *kensho*, a word variously understood as 'seeing one's true nature', satori, or enlightenment.

Every few weeks those who attend a *zendo* will see the teacher in a private interview known as *dokusan*. Here Sister Elaine is at her richest, her wisdom and compassion most apparent. She can be stern and gentle, sometimes both at once, as she throws out sometimes quite extraordinary questions with a directness and humour that conceal the depth of their implications. Often these sessions are baffling, but it is surprising how often, for me usually on the way home, one catches oneself thinking, 'Oh *yes*, that's what she meant.' What goes on in these interviews is both esoteric and private, but she is on record as admitting that she does not give much encouragement as 'sitting is its own reward'.

Even though meditation is today practised by many people, there are still some who consider it self-indulgent, suggesting that it is somehow opposed to caring for others. Sister Elaine gave the lie to this on the very first day I went to her *zendo*. She told us that her teacher Yamada Roshi used to say: 'If we do not shed tears for those who are crying, then there has been no *kensho* at all.' She often says that after sitting, meditators should be 'shot off their cushions into the world of greed, anger and ignorance, injustice, poverty and pollution'. And of course she herself practises this, in her work as Director of the Prison Phoenix Trust, where prisoners learn to turn their cell from a place of confinement to a place of freedom. One man wrote, 'The past year has been the most meaningful, most real, of my life. As I sit here now, although I'm in prison, I'm free. Who could ever imagine a man's freedom being found in prison?' Another man, imprisoned by the Marcos regime in the Philippines, said, 'Now I know that where I am and where I want to be are no different at all! The bars and stone walls do not really separate me from my loved ones, from my friends, from my people, from everything and everybody in the universe . . . I am perfectly free, I am perfectly happy, and deeply at peace.'

The name Elaine comes from Helen, meaning 'Bright light of the sun'. For seven decades that light was to get brighter, and in 1981, when Yamada Roshi gave Sister Elaine her Zen name, he chose *Ko-un Ang*, meaning 'Cloud of Light'. He knew her well. Perhaps in this naming he was anticipating her work for Zen, for he knew too that the Sanskrit for light originally meant 'the keeper of the holy flame.' Zen is about light, about seeing things as they really are. It is also about living in the present, experiencing fully at all times, being 'electrically charged'. Sister Elaine herself is the best advertisement for her teaching. If you cannot meet her, at least read her book.

Shirley du Boulay
Oxford, October 1995

Introduction

This little book has gone through three previous editions. It was first presented in 1986 as one of a twin set by the Zen Center, Philippines, to mark its tenth anniversary. Together with its companion volume *Total Liberation: Zen Spirituality and the Social Dimension* by Ruben Habito, they were meant to parallel the twin Zen components of *Wisdom and Compassion*. Slightly revised, the two books were combined in 1990 and entitled *The Zen Experience in a Philippine Context*.

In 1993, the Theosophical Society of the Philippines printed a version of my original text for worldwide distribution, under the title *Teaching Zen to Christians*. It was this version that came into the hands of HarperCollins*Publishers*, who wanted to publish the text with two additional chapters, one autobiographical and the other on spirituality, which form this present volume. The editor's wish was to underscore the Christian participation, since there are many 'how to' books on Zen from the Buddhist point of view. So, this is the account of how a Zen teacher, who is a practising Christian, teaches the basics of Zen practice not only without jeopardy to one's Christianity, but also reveals how this gem of Buddhism can enhance one's Christian spirituality. Robert Kennedy put it very succinctly in a recent talk, calling it 'the challenge of being an honest broker of both traditions'.[1]

The present text is almost identical to the text used in the Philippines, where the people's spirituality is Oriental (there is still influence derived from their pre-Christian religion) but where they nevertheless accepted Christianity wholeheartedly. I would like to say, though, for my English readers, that the orientation talks I give here in Britain use Christian references somewhat less. It is rather difficult to gauge the temperature of religious feelings here, and after three years I am still finding my way. But first perhaps it would be timely to say a few words about how the book got started in the first place.

Since Vatican II, a Catholic missioner no longer goes to a non-Christian country only to proselytize. Our new mandate is to enter into dialogue and discover the 'ray of truth' to be found in all the world's great religions. This dialogue also finds expression in all religions working together to solve the world's problems with the environment, towards the eradication of poverty and pollution, as well as the pursuit of peace and justice through sustainable development.

I went to Japan in 1961, four years before the promulgation of Vatican II. Having been trained as a violinist, I discerned that the best possible path for me as a missioner would be to share what I could of Western classical music, for which the Japanese have a great hunger and appreciation, in exchange for learning the beauties and truths in Buddhism's great gift to the world, the Way of Zen.

After completing my language school requirements, we opened the Suita Culture Centre, and also I began Zen practice with the Rinzai Zen Buddhist nuns at Enkoji Temple in Kyoto. Eight years later, I became a disciple of Yamada Koun Roshi, of the Sanbo Kyodan (literally 'The Three Treasures Teaching Group') in Kamakura. Eventually, I was given permission to teach.

Shortly after going to the Philippines in 1976, I was asked to set up a Zen Centre for the Catholic Church there. Two years later, the Asian Bishops met in Bangalore, India, and deploring the breakdown of Asia's spiritual values, encouraged the use of Asian prayer forms and the establishing of ashrams and *zendos*. So my primary work in the Philippines was to bring the Way of Zen, learned at the feet of a strict Japanese Buddhist master, into the already rich storehouse of Christian spirituality. I found this a most exciting endeavour.

First of all I would like to say that I have found the Eastern and Western meditation practices to be quite different, and I use both daily. During orientation, parallels are frequently drawn between Western and Oriental spiritualities, and this has been one of my delights. I hasten to say that I am not a theologian and therefore do not pretend to teach that one equals the other. As I said, I see them as quite different, although most certainly leading to the same focus. In fact, after being in this discipline for over thirty years, I am daily more convinced that each complements the other. But that is for others to discover themselves.

And so it has been my ongoing overview and joy as a missioner to present to Christians the beauty and truth of Zen, kept alive for centuries in certain streams of the Buddhist religion. But it was a surprise to be told when I was still in the Philippines by Vicente Hao Chin that the Theosophical Society wanted to publish this book, not because of its presentation of Zen, but rather as an exposition of contemporary Catholicism!

Through necessity, the Zen introductory talks are based on the orientation as given at the mother *zendo* in Japan, the San-un Zendo in Kamakura. Because many of his disciples were not Buddhist, our teacher Yamada Koun Roshi would frequently supplement the Buddhist vocabulary with a variety of words which pointed to the unnamable and indescribable Reality in more philosophical terms. This helped our Western-trained minds to become unstuck from specific words and concepts, as we determined to enter the world of experience, specifically to come to the Zen experience of *kensho*, or seeing that great Reality as one's own nature. Our Christian articulation of that experience and its environment can only be done by us Christians, the Roshi used to counsel. What follows in the main text is such an attempt by one of his disciples.

Since it is our intention here to acquaint Christians with a Buddhist practice, the terminology used for orientation would naturally use some Buddhist terms. Born Catholics in the very faith-filled Church of the Philippines had moments of apprehension when dealing with some of the Buddhist articulations. So I endeavoured to ease the fear by drawing a Christian parallel within my own experience. Frequently there is also resort to Japanese terms, and in so doing, nothing esoteric is meant. Where the English equivalent fits exactly, we use the English word. If Japanese is used, it usually means we are teaching something new and perhaps unique to Zen.

There is also nothing official or final here. I feel it is far too early in religious history to have Zen comfortably situated in Western religious and cultural terms. But we *are* at a particular point in history which is what this book is all about. Let us first, though, look at the background of what we have inherited.

The historian Professor Arnold Toynbee once said that the meeting of Buddhism and Christianity would be one of the most important events in the twentieth century. This book concerns part of that encounter. It is about Zen, the current contemplative practice in Mahayana Zen Buddhism.

Zen is nonconceptual and is neither theology nor philosophy. Rather, Zen points directly to the heart-mind and does not rely on words and letters. In practice, this pointing ripens into experience in a touch which transforms as it awakens. The Buddhist term for that which we perceive is Buddha Nature. My teacher more often used the term Essential Nature, or the Empty-Infinite. Some of the ancient Chinese masters referred to it as

Original Nature. Zen is a direct and living transmission, from an enlightened teacher to an enlightened disciple.

Traditionally, in Zen as practised in Japan, orientation was not given to the neophyte. One could only demonstrate a sincere desire to learn by presenting oneself at the monastery gate and waiting in a posture of humble supplication. This period could last up to seven days, although food was usually left beside the petitioner at regular intervals. Once admitted into the monastery, it was a matter of time and experience until the seeker came to understand what Zen is about. This could take a long time indeed.

About fifty years ago, Harada Daiun Roshi (1871–1961), perhaps the most influential Japanese Zen master to appear in the first half of this century, started giving explanatory talks to beginners in Zen. He belonged to the *Soto* lineage, one of the two main branches of Zen Buddhism in Japan. Unable to find a truly accomplished master within his own tradition, Harada Roshi undertook intensive study with teachers from the other major Zen sect, which is *Rinzai*. Upon returning to his own monastery as a full-fledged Zen master, Harada Roshi combined the best of *Soto* and *Rinzai* into an independent stream of Zen which later became the Sanbo Kyodan.

Harada Roshi also broke with tradition in orientation; feeling that the modern mind was so much more aware and knowledgeable, he felt it appropriate to give group orientation talks. The practice was continued by his successor, Yasutani Hakuun Roshi (1885–1973) and later by my teacher, Yamada Koun Roshi, who headed the San-un Zendo (Three Clouds Zendo) in Kamakura, the headquarters of the Sanbo Kyodan, until his death in 1989.

It was to Yamada Roshi, a free-spirited and gifted teacher, that not only many seekers who were Buddhist, but also lay Christians, priests and sisters from all over the world came to study authentic Zen. To many of them, Yamada Roshi would say: 'I will teach you to be better Christians.' And he did.

There is a current malaise afflicting many Western Christians of whatever denomination. Church gatherings still have some appeal for those of a charismatic or traditionalist bent, but since the early sixties, and despite the *aggiornamento* of Vatican II, the number of churchgoers in Europe and America has been steadily declining.

The roots of this phenomenon are undoubtedly complex, but I think they are generally contained in a greater phenomenon that is sweeping the world today, the massive shift in consciousness towards a new paradigm. Change has become the order of the day, and many predict the emergence of a new world-view, one that is rooted in a different perception of reality.

This new paradigm will necessitate a marked change or at least a more holistic approach to spirituality. It will have to present an alternative vision of reality from the one that has dominated our perception for centuries. This will undoubtedly necessitate sloughing off layers of accumulated baggage, and the evolution of a spirituality that is faithful to our universal unity.

A friend whose name appears often in the following pages, the late Fr Hugo Enomiya-Lassalle, says in his last book *Living in the New Consciousness*[2] that the new paradigm will bring with it a transformation of consciousness into a kind of mystical knowing, in which reality is perceived to its very essence. In this way we shall come to experience holistically, overcoming the more extreme forms of dualism. He holds out the Way of Zen as evolving into this new stage.

Zen itself transcends religion and race, and nationality and gender. Mahayana (large vehicle) Zen existed not only in India and China, but also in Tibet, Vietnam and Korea. One often hears comments on the differences between the 'kinds' of Zen that evolved in different countries and cultures. For instance,

Indian Zen is said to be philosophical, Chinese Zen more earthy and poetic, and Japanese Zen pragmatic.

One must remember, however, that in those days, countries were very much isolated from outside influence. As we approach the twenty-first century, we may take it for granted that worldwide communication is almost instantaneous, and the possibility of nations recognizing their identity as well as their interdependence, makes a kind of universal Zen more probable. The work of colleagues and myself in bringing Zen to other nations and religions and cultures is not so difficult in the practice itself. The problems arise when one attempts to write a book about the whole procedure, for Zen just experiences and does not give explanations.

The Sanbo Kyodan remains the present matrix for those who trained under Yamada Koun Roshi. He left about a dozen teachers, who are running *zendos* in many countries around the world. The present leader is Kubota Ji-un Roshi, who is ably assisted by the former *roshi*'s elder son, Yamada Ryoun Roshi. They hold *sesshin* (retreat) at various Zen centres affiliated with the Sanbo Kyodan, but principally in Japan at the San-un Zendo in Kamakura.

To all of its disciples deemed to have trodden the Path, the Sanbo Kyodan gives confirmation to their teachers, whatever the nationality, religion, culture or gender. The only demand is that they remain in true transmission in their teaching, and sensitive to the needs of living peacefully and productively in today's world. The Way of Zen as outlined in this book is not only a means of helping us through this period of paradigm change, but if Fr Lassalle's prediction stands, we will find ourselves to have been there already, when we arrive!

Elaine MacInnes
Oxford, November 1995

At one point in her study, Sister Elaine asked Yamada Roshi what he thought prayer should be for a Christian. His immediate response was,

'It should be the same as for a Buddhist. Prayer is light sitting in light.'

CHAPTER ONE

Silencing the Body to Harmony

The art of silence

What is Zen? Where did the name come from and what does it mean? Zen as we know it today is said to come to us from China. The Chinese made no attempt to change the sound of the word *dhyana* when Bodhidharma brought Zen to their country from India. And the ideogram they chose to write the word in their language is a combination of the characters for 'infinite' and 'simple' with the intimation of 'offering'. The quiet sitting, which was probably the tradition they received from India, changed but perhaps not radically when it met Chinese Taoism. There are also some enduring signs of Confucian influence to be found.

The Way of Zen is in silencing the body and mind by means of a specific posture and breath absorption while we are on the *zafu* (a small, round sitting cushion), and what the Buddhists call an awareness of being in our daily lives. Zen is a discipline which acts therapeutically and builds up *joriki* (literally a settling power) which leads eventually to a specific religious experience. History teaches us that as a result of having that experience, Zen monks were urged on to external expressions of compassion.

One of the best biblical quotations for introducing the Way of Zen to a Christian is the well-known line from Psalm 46, 'Be still and know that I am God.' Oriental teachers would have us take that advice literally. Biblical scholars tell us that the Hebrew verb 'to know' is *yadah* which also means 'to experience'. So even the Christian Bible tells us to be still, be silent, and we will come to experience God.

Silence is an art we in the twentieth century have pretty much lost. Perhaps because it is such a rare commodity, many people today are seeking it, and finding it is not as easy as turning off the television or taking drugs. Silence is a practice in the widest sense of the word. It helps to maintain peace of mind during the ups and downs of daily living. When it visibly contributes to our wellbeing, we take it as a way of life. Many psychiatrists are of the opinion that we wouldn't need any doctors at all, if the mind were at rest.

Because an overactive mind is the dis-ease of the century, it is not uncommon for spiritual seekers to forsake all and travel to the ends of the earth to find a true teacher, one in legitimate transmission, but who nevertheless knows what's going on in the minds and hearts of people today. The contemporary seeker may not be kept waiting at a gate to gain admission, but will be expected to demonstrate a willingness to learn, listening not only to the teacher and to one's own body and mind, but indeed to the universe itself, and all the ten thousand things in it.

Beginners today are cautioned to:

1. Allow themselves to be emptied.
2. Let go, so they will have no fear of emptiness.
3. Give up their busy-ness, which is often a state of mind or habit.

In today's world, psychologists warn that we often exhaust our mind in egotistical pursuits, a mind already alienated by an illusory fear of separation. The antidote is living life in awareness and then eventually coming to 'see' that indeed, that which binds all the world together is One and we are in and of that Oneness. There is no separation, and things are just as they are as we see in the following verse from the *Mumonkan*:

> The spring flowers, the moon in autumn,
> The cool breezes of summer, the winter's snow.
> If idle concerns do not cloud the mind
> This is our happiest season.[3]

Silence is the shaft we descend to the depths of contemplation. Silence is the vehicle that takes us to the innermost centre of our being which is the place for all authentic practice. Ruben Habito, a contemporary Christian Zen teacher, friend and mentor, once identified Zen as 'an invitation to experience where God dwells'.

Real silence is prayer. The spiritual traditions of both East and West attest to this, although the Western voice has been somewhat blurred for centuries. In the old days we frequently heard the chant *silentium tibi laus* – silence is the highest and truest praise of God. That being so, I think *zazen* will eventually find an appropriate niche in Christianity.

Lao Tzu tells us that silence is the great revelation. What does it tell us? Well, many things along the way in daily transformation, and eventually it reveals the Self. When we come to know this True Self, we come to know who we are. In his book *Prayer* Abhishiktananda (Dom Henri Saux) says something to the effect that to experience the Self is the highest possible attainment for a human being.

While in Kamakura, I frequently did some interpreting for Yamada Roshi when young Americans and Europeans had their first interview. When asked why they wanted to do *zazen*, most replied 'to find out who I am'. Lack of identity and the sense of alienation is indeed prevalent in today's world.

For expediency, we speak of daily transformation and the discovery of Self separately, although they are not two. We learn through sitting that they coalesce. Zen masters would applaud the words of Catherine of Siena: 'All the way to heaven is heaven itself, because Christ said, "I am the Way." ' Christ for the Christian is both means and end.

There are many ways to meditate. There are several kinds of prayer that teach us how to be silent. There are also many kinds of prayer that increase the noise. Zazen is one of the ways of practising silence, an art which the Orient never really lost.

Zazen

How do we practice the Way of silence? The core of Zen practice is zazen, or sitting meditation. Zazen is a discipline in which we silence and harmonize the body and mind and breath, which acts first of all therapeutically, and eventually, when all things are ready, effects a specific spiritual experience.

The word zazen is written in Japanese with two ideograms. The first is za, which means 'to sit'; and the second is zen from the Sanskrit dhyana, usually translated 'meditation'. In the Orient, meditation goes beyond intellect, feeling, memory and imagination to a deeper level of consciousness.

It is with the first syllable, za 'to sit on the floor', that this chapter concerns itself. Generally speaking, for sitting we follow the age-old practice of yoga, which is to assume a stable, balanced posture, a straight spine, and the breath moving in and out of the lungs freely. However, there are some ways in which we in Zen differ from yogic sitting. Primarily we use two cushions: the zabuton, a large square cushion which acts as a buffer for the knees and ankles; and the zafu, a small round cushion which rests atop the zabuton and lifts and supports the spine. Both cushions are well stuffed with kapok, as they need to be firm.

Preliminaries

First: Wear clean and comfortable baggy clothing, so as not to constrict blood vessels that supply the muscles with much-needed oxygen and nourishment. When sitting with others, clothing should be a quiet shade of unfigured material. Vivid colours like red, and brightly printed patterns, are distracting and eye-catching and therefore unsuitable for *zendo* use.

Second: Sit the way you can. There are six positions available so try to become proficient in several. You will then find relief in changing position when you participate in long hours of *sesshin* (zen retreat). *Zazen* is neither punishment nor asceticism. It is well situated within the area of discipline, so sit the way you can. It is also advisable to do appropriate exercises, particularly to loosen the groin. Depending on age and other such factors, you will gradually become proficient in several positions, including the full lotus.

Third: In most positions, there are three points of body contact with the *zabuton*. Usually these are the two knees and the buttocks. They must form a solid tripod. If you cannot make the contact points, then insert a small auxiliary cushion to fill in the space, between the knee and the floor. These three points need a lot of support, otherwise the body will be wobbly. Yamada Roshi used to quote Dogen Zenji: 'Sit like a mountain.' A mountain is a solid mass and has a good broad base.

Fourth: In sitting, the central part of the body is of course the back, which must receive special attention. The normal curve of the spine is retained. After arranging your legs in the desired position, make movements of gradually decreasing arcs from left to right, until the spine naturally comes to rest in the upright position. Then lean forward once, extending the flesh of the buttocks backwards. Return to the upright position, leaving the buttocks extended.

In the dojo (the place of practice), the people monitoring are constantly correcting back positions. What we do with the spine in sitting is of utmost importance. Good posture helps our *zazen*. The popular Indian Jesuit, the late Anthony de Mello, used to say that slouching brings distractions. A bad sitting posture can also contribute to spinal distress, one of the world's most common physical complaints today. It has been said that our spinal column was originally designed so that we could swing gracefully in trees. That is a long way from sitting upright on cushions, sedentary for many hours. Doctors tell us that lack of exercise, bad posture and obesity are the most prevalent causes of back trouble, and advocate daily exercise, weight loss and posture correction, as well as a firm mattress and bedboard for sleeping.

For daily living today, exercise is indispensable, and we applaud the current physical fitness enthusiasm with its emphasis on conditioning, proper weight, and diet. There are many excellent exercise programmes to be found. Being in the field of Oriental spirituality, we tend to stress yoga and/or one of the variations of *T'ai Chi*.

Whatever your programme, see that it includes the whole body, and is in harmony with the psyche and Spirit. The exercises we use in *sesshin* are naturally designed to help us sit more easily, so they concern mostly the legs and hips. They are to be done with breath awareness. With correct posture and proper cushions, the blood vessels are free to bring oxygen and nourishment to the muscles and carry off wastes. However, sitting does tend to slacken the abdominal muscle tone, and as one grows older, a potbelly develops, which puts added pressure on the spine. This points to an added need for exercise and proper posture to remedy this tendency. Lower back pain is a warning that something is wrong, do not disregard it. If you have pain when you sit, be sure to tell your teacher.

Leg positions

Full Lotus: Seat yourself on the front third of the *zafu*. Put the right foot on the left thigh and the left foot on the right thigh. Draw the heels up to the abdomen, but leave the toes free to wiggle. This position is the most difficult, but also the best because there is the least distortion to the spine. It is obviously the most symmetrical.

Half-Lotus: Tuck the right foot under the left thigh and place the left foot on top of the right thigh. This position is the most used by the majority of sitters. It is only partially symmetrical. Compensate for this by adjusting the round *zafu* under your torso, until the spine is as upright as possible. You may also put the left foot under the right thigh, and the right foot on top of the left thigh. This position may require a slightly higher *zafu*.

Burmese: Draw the right foot up close to the left thigh or vice versa, allowing the foot, calf and knee to rest on the *zabuton*. Then place the left leg in front of the right, so that both knees touch the cushion. This requires a still higher *zafu*. Adjust positioning of the body carefully, paying particular attention to the spine.

Kneeler: Tuck a kneeler under the thighs and sit on it. A kneeler is a small wooden bench and can be used to relieve a lot of the leg pressure in sitting. A thin cushion on top of the kneeler is helpful.

Seiza: With knees apart, put a high thick *zafu* between the heels. Lower the buttocks well over the *zafu*. Adjust the hips until comfortably seated. This is a position often used in Japan for ordinary quiet sitting.

Chair: Beginners are generally reluctant to use a chair for sitting. It may however be the best way to sit temporarily until you get in shape for floor sitting. For older people with permanent disabilities, it may always be the best position. A flat stool or chair not upholstered is preferable. Place a *zafu* on the seat and sit on the front third as directed above. The feet are flat on the floor, shoulder-width apart and the legs of the chair should be adjusted so that the knees are slightly lower than the hips. Straighten the spine and do not lean against the back of the chair. An adjustable piano stool would be ideal.

Mudra

While sitting in *zazen*, the hand position has always been considered to be of utmost importance, and is called the mudra. Mudra is a Sanskrit word which means 'seal', and refers to physical gestures, especially hand movements, which are meant to evoke certain states of mind. In the *zazen* mudra the right hand rests palm up on the sitter's lap, the left hand is placed on top of the right hand, and the two thumb tips touch lightly, so that the hands form an oval shape. They are then drawn towards the navel. The actual placement of the hands will vary according to the leg position used. For instance, in the full lotus, the hands will rest on the heels. In all positions, let the arms relax as much as possible.

Many beginners ask to sit with their hands on the knees. We insist on the zen mudra. Several Japanese acupuncturists went to study in China after it opened its doors to the world. They returned home exclaiming they now understood why Zen sitters use the mudra for it connects energy cycles that course through the meridians of the body.

Eyes and mouth

The eyes are lowered to a spot on the floor, about one metre directly in front of the nose. They are open, seeing but not looking, and resting on the spot. They will not necessarily remain in focus. The mouth is closed, but the teeth are not biting, and the tip of the tongue is resting against the upper front teeth. This helps prevent over-salivating.

Breathing

In the Ways of the Orient, we read a lot about breathing. Even in Zen, there is sometimes a mistaken notion that we should breathe deeply from the abdomen. Yamada Roshi explained that this was widely used in Japan during a period when there was much poverty and many monks had tuberculosis. Breathing cold air would irritate their lungs and cause fits of coughing. It was Hakuin Zenji who experimented with using the lower cavities of the lungs when breathing. He referred to this as breathing from the abdomen and it was successful in stopping the coughing. This was only an historical expediency for a dojo with many sick monks.

At our Zen Center, we give very simple instructions for breathing. First of all, breathe naturally. Whatever is natural for you, do just that. All Oriental disciplines begin by being breath-centred, and as you breathe in and out in one-pointed concentration, the breath naturally becomes a little slower and deeper, unconsciously. But if your breathing is unnatural, you will over-aspirate and become dizzy and the body will wobble.

9

All Dogen Zenji says about breathing is to put the breath gently in the nose.

Practice

In the wide sense, the word 'practice' is usually associated with Oriental disciplines and designates the spiritual path on which we pattern our daily life. In a narrower sense, we often hear 'Zen is my practice.' And in an even more particular sense, teachers frequently ask 'what is your practice in Zen?' implying that there are several 'things' one can be doing whilst sitting on the zafu. Christianity's parallel word seems to be 'spirituality', which in recent years is being used even outside religious circles. In my present work with the Prison Phoenix Trust in Oxford where we encourage prisoners to practise yoga and meditation, spirituality is seen as the inner workings of the spirit first in body and mind, and then in daily life. The book will conclude with an outline of what is perhaps a total spirituality today, but in this chapter the reference will be only to the Way of Zen.

In giving a practice to beginners during the several weeks of orientation, we concentrate on what could be called mind training exercises. Most people who come to us for orientation know that in Zen one stops the thinking process, but there is no real comprehension of what that entails. We liken it to contemplation, but since that word does not as yet enjoy a very specific connotation, we find it helpful at this stage to add that John of the Cross also sees contemplation as the cessation of sense and spiritual faculties. Specifically, we endeavour to stop linear thinking, even to avoid entertaining random thoughts, and all such mental activities as feeling, remembering, imagining and planning, etc. In other words, we disengage the psyche from all its busyness. For people living in the hub of today's world, this is a shift of gargantuan magnitude.

The first practice we give beginners is counting the breaths. When seated appropriately on the *zafu*, watch the breath come in and out for a few sequences, and then start counting the breaths from one to ten. The inhalations will be the odd numbers and the exhalations the even. Breathe the way that is natural for you, count only to ten. Higher mathematics require the use of the intellect and memory!

Counting the breaths may sound easy, but in practice it is quite difficult to do just that, without being distracted from the count by stray thoughts, memories, fantasies, etc. When your mind wanders, perhaps to the point of losing the count altogether, simply resume counting from one. You will probably notice that the exhalation is longer than the inhalation, and that there is a considerable period of time when we seem to do neither. Thus we gradually gain a little control of our superactive mind through the very simple expediency of breath-counting. One *roshi* friend said he had a beginner who never got past number one in his counting! And it may not be appropriate to call breath-counting a mind training exercise for beginners. For some it will be a lifetime practice.

In the zendo, we sit without moving for a 25-minute period, followed by a 5-minute walking meditation which we call *kinhin*. We do *kinhin* by fisting the right hand and covering it lightly with the left, keeping the eyes focused on a spot about two metres ahead or on the back of the person in front. We walk at a slow pace, set by the monitor. *Kinhin* is designed solely for flexing muscles and tendons and reactivating sluggish blood vessels.

Until we can sit that 25 minutes, the beginner's endurance decides the timing of the sits. Many sitters start with a 15-minute span, followed by a 5-minute *kinhin*, then another 15-minute sit, etc. Gradually one reaches the required 25-minute stretch, and the individual or orientation group is then invited to join the *sangha* (community of practitioners) in its regular sittings. All beginners are urged to sit regularly every day for at least one-half hour or, better still, one regular sit in the morning and one in the evening. For most of us, that hour after first arising in the morning is by far the best time for *zazen*. Remember: no thoughts, no concepts, no feelings, just breath-awareness and breath-counting.

General Points

Orientation talks appeal to the intellect, but there is not much in Zen that is intellectual. Real Zen activity happens at another level, and the power to reach that level is usually generated on your cushion. Neither words of instruction nor inspiration, no matter how eloquent, can reach that level.

True Zen cannot be understood intellectually. Zen is not going anywhere or doing anything. One definition of Zen is that it is experiencing fully at all times. It has to be practised and experienced to be understood.

Zen is a process and although uninteresting, some people do persevere in its practice for years. The fact that the zendo is crowded each week is an indication that something is happening to the people sitting. You may come rather soon to the point where you experience feeling better on the days you sit. Your mind will gradually shed its shackles and eventually attain peace, because you will have disciplined yourself to let go of attitudes and preconceived ideas. That peace is the beginning of harmony.

Sitting with others is also part of Zen. When people sit together, there is an added something that happens in conjunction with all present. This is by way of warning that you will find it difficult to sit alone. But everyone has to learn to cope with that problem.

Do not waste time on your cushion. Many of us lead very busy lives, and sitting still for 30 minutes presents a great temptation to catch up with planning. Determine to just sit during the time allotted for *zazen*. Be faithful to this daily practice, and don't get bogged down with unanswered questions. Only gradually and when you are ready, will everything fall into place. In the meantime, you have started on a Way that will soon be paying dividends in your daily life.

One last point has to do with moving along the Zen process rather quickly. It is beyond the power of a teacher to ascertain how long a beginner will take to experience what Zen has to offer, for the pace differs with each individual. Some advance very quickly, and soon come to a deep state of sitting. At such a time, there are certain phenomena that can be experienced, which may be visual, aural, or physical body sensations.

Ultimately, these are of no consequence and are to be ignored, but they nevertheless indicate a degree of the sitter's progress and should be reported to the teacher. They are called *makyo* (representations from the subconscious) and a more adequate presentation will be given later. Suffice it here to say that sitting puts us in touch with areas deep in the psyche. This often results in a flow of tears. There is no cause for alarm as they are often external manifestations of an inner healing process. Tears and/or *makyo* should always be reported and then forgotten. They are on no account to be cultivated.

CHAPTER TWO

Silencing the Mind to Harmony

After putting the body in the best position for silence, we then do the same for the mind. The Oriental way of achieving this is not to activate the psyche. This process starts with breath-awareness, for beginners, counting the breaths. 'Every effort at doing this paves the way for the spirit within to return to its original spontaneity' as one of the ancient Chinese masters phrased it.

On our cushion, we do the practice assigned by the teacher, which at this stage is breath-counting. Away from the cushion, we are aware of being. By that is meant that we are where we are, and we do what we are doing. For instance, if we are washing the dishes, our body and mind are absorbed in harmony while performing that task. We so often practise separation by allowing our mind to wander where it will, when we're doing some non-intellectual work such as washing dishes.

Of course there is no problem when we're doing intellectually or artistically absorbing work. If we are solving geometrical problems, we just solve them. But when we put them aside, and go out to sweep leaves, we so often still keep doing geometry in our heads. There is something about Western culture that encourages and praises this. In Oriental spirituality it is frowned upon, because in this way we are separating mind and body.

Separation is the arch-enemy of all life. Indeed the word

'diabolical' is from the Greek *diaballein*, to separate or divide. So separation is the work of the devil, and let us away with it. In all our waking moments, let us try to be where we are, and not separated from the work or play in which we are engaged. When we complete one task, we drop it cleanly and proceed to the next encounter, in awareness.

As Christians in prayer, we are not unused to silencing ourselves away from our work whether physical or mental, as we relate to the transcendental God through mind and heart, memory and imagination. This is our tradition and is as old as Christendom, and beyond as well. We are rational beings, and the relationship is nourishing for both mind and heart. It is our invaluable heritage, attested to eloquently in Western art, culture, and religions. But we also have the heritage of contemplation, with little or no use of words, of the great doctor of Christian prayer, John of the Cross, and Meister Eckhart, and Tauler and many others.

Zen is a state of consciousness beyond subject and object, and therefore not dual or relational. I used to feel the word 'communion' was apt in describing Zen prayer, but now I feel perhaps 'participation' is closer to what's happening, where one's whole being is unimpededly as it were, infused with the Divine.

However, when I entered the convent in 1953, it was almost impossible to find a teacher for guidance in contemplation. At best, one is told that mystical prayer is God's gift and one can only ask for it. I was fortunate enough to find a book which kept me on the path. I had to come to the Orient to learn that there are teachers in this Way and there is a practice, which will lead to mystical experience, although the experience itself is 'a gift from beyond' as Dogen Zenji implied.

The first step for a Christian doing Zen is to agree to leave behind the world of subject and object. No books are helpful in this kind of meditation, for when we grab one in the chapel or our place of prayer, we are just exchanging objects. We have, for the time being, to stop living in the head, because there, we are living in the past or future. The Orient tells us that now is the only reality, for the past has gone and the future will never come. All we have is here and now.

The whole of Zen discipline is to make us come alive to the present. When we are sitting, we concentrate on our breathing. Away from the cushion, we are one with our activity.

In *zazen*, breath-awareness is the preliminary, and can sweep away thoughts. *Be* the breathing in and out. Not to think but to *be*, is the secret of Zen. Relax and enjoy your breathing, though be in awe. We have Scripture's word that it is the *Ruah*, the breath of God. I understand there is a Filipino saying, 'When we die, God's breath is taken back.' In the meantime, let us marvel at the mystery that 'we are'!

As we advance in awareness of being, and gain some control over our active mind whilst we sit, gradually stillness and a certain equanimity take over. Very soon we feel better on the days we meditate, and more scattered if for some reason or other, we cannot sit.

The therapeutic effects of mature sitting are well known. Our dissipated energies gradually become more unified and we really start to gain some control over our superactive mind. Tensions are released, nerves become unfrayed, and physical health generally improves. Emotions are sensitized and the will strengthened. We begin to experience a kind of inner balance and gradually dryness, rigidity, hang-ups, prejudices and egotism melt and give way to compassion, serenity, egolessness and social concern. This is transformation indeed, although it does not happen the week after we start sitting. It is a lifelong endeavour.

There seems to be a general inherent expectation of transformation in prayer. It has been my experience over the last 35 years that more significant changes in the psyche occur in the practice of meditation than in prayers of petition. This is not to denigrate the same factor in relational prayer which uses the psyche and can promote change there. We certainly feel better after a heart-to-heart talk with the Lord, though many Christian prayer leaders place the cause of the present-day crisis in faith precisely in this area. In all Jesuit retreat houses in the Philippines, one could find notes by the American Jesuit Armand Nigro to the effect that there is no hope for improvement unless individual persons begin to respond better to God in prayer.

Personality changes are also effected by Zen. It may be a prayer of the desert, but perhaps that is where changes occur after all. We cannot expect to mature spiritually if we keep our prayer at the objective stage, and accompany it with words. Thoughts and feelings hold inordinate sway over us and using the imagination is now very popular in the alternative disciplines and therapies. They are all much warmer and colourful than the desert. But prayer will not normally produce transforming results as long as it is in the 'doing and saying' stage. It is the inner power of the Spirit in the dynamic unifying silence that changes us.

That we can commune with God in silence and call it prayer is new for most Christians today. Although there is a growing distrust of verbiage, there is still some discomfort with total silence. In an unpublished manuscript, the late Fr Lassalle said:

Taking a quick look at our contemporaries, we find ourselves living in a world of change. The new stage will bring with it the new person. In it, we will have a new approach to our faith. We are already seeing the result, that in the West where rationale has for centuries been overstressed, the aspect of tradition has become a hindrance to faith today. Religion and faith are not things only to be understood and/or explained. The religious person's faith today is not fed by arguments and tradition. We are coming more and more to seek an experience in faith. This in turn is revolutionizing our prayer life. Object meditation is becoming so unpopular that there is even some question as to the validity of starting beginners with it.

It may be interesting to note here, that in many Oriental countries, prayer is started at the super-object stage. This is particularly true of those countries that have had the least contact with the West. Occidentals are today aware of a strong new trend to the mysticism which is an experience of God. Now this is exactly the supra-object meditation which leads to an experience of faith and God. Any present exposé of the new person's spirituality which misses this point is drawing but a partial profile. People calling themselves Christians today must be prepared to expect an attraction to prayer in depth and not on the surface.

Now let us consider the Japanese ideograms of *zazen*, and where and when it was first found. In an ordinary dictionary, the meaning of *za* is given as 'to sit'. The kind of sitting it refers to is squatting on the floor. As said before, the body is of utmost importance in *zazen*, and it is true that our body participates when we sit. Western Christianity has, unfortunately, been locked into Greek thought patterns for centuries, in which the body was considered a mere shell for the superior spirit.

Jungian friends say that the works of Carl Jung have helped many Christians to recognize the integral role of body and psyche in the evolution of consciousness and spiritual development. Over the years, the importance of the body is gaining recognition in the West, and in the Orient, it is of sufficient importance that the meditation is most frequently referred to as 'sitting'.

As stated previously, the other ideogram *zen* uses 'infinite' 'simple' and connoting 'offering', which may give adequate explanation of its meaning. The word *zen* involves the Chinese sound-adaptation of the Sanskrit *dhyana* and was pronounced 'channa' or 'chan'. When the Japanese came to China, their pronunciation of the Chinese sounded like 'zenna' or 'zen'.

The beginning of *zazen* is lost in antiquity. Scholars say the word *dhyana* can be found in the Vedic books of ancient India, which were completed about 1500 BC. The practice itself certainly predates the Vedas, and recent archaeological discoveries indicate that the practice of sitting may have begun several millennia earlier.

Dhyana certainly sprang into new prominence following the enlightenment experience of Siddhartha Gautama, who was born about 654 BC in what is now Nepal. He was the first-born of the king and queen of the tribe of Shakya. He led a very sheltered and rather pampered life for some years, totally unaware, it seems, of life's realities for the majority of his father's people.

Gradually the young man experienced a desire to witness what was going on beyond the palace gates, and in company with a wise teacher, he set forth and encountered the darker side of the world. To his great consternation, he saw old age and sickness and even witnessed a funeral procession. For the first time in his life he was confronted with poverty, suffering and death. He returned home a frightened and changed man.

In time he became obsessed with the problem of suffering. Why is there suffering? Why? It became his *koan*, and hounded him relentlessly until he eventually took leave of his kingdom and wife and young son, and set out on a journey to find the answer.

First he turned to philosophy, which was highly sophisticated at that time in India. However, all its subtleties could not tell him why there was suffering. Then he went to the forest and sought the company of the zealous ascetics. He lived with them for six years, it is said, denying himself sufficient food and sleep and clothing, until his body was wasted and weak, and his mind and heart discouraged. Still his 'why' remained a mystery.

In answer to prayer, he abandoned asceticism and took food. With restored vigour, he decided that the only way to grapple with the problem was to grapple with himself. He determined to sit in meditation under the pipal tree, which after his enlightenment became known as the *bodhi* tree, until he solved his *koan* (pronounced ko-ahn) which is a conundrum that baffles the intellect.

Gradually he began to feel that he was on the right path. More and more he came to see that he and his quest were not two different things. Finally, we are told in Buddhist scriptures, at the age of 29, on 8 December (by the Japanese calendar) while watching the twinkling of the morning star, his inner world exploded and disappeared. His question vanished, too, and then he *knew* (*satorimashita* ... verb form of *satori* 'to know'). He awakened to his own inner reality which he experienced as not being separate from the great reality of the cosmos, a happening that was both exhilarating and liberating. The Great Matter of the Oriental Nothingness. The Nothingness that is All.

In Zen orientation, the teacher at this point will mention the word *Tathagata* which Shakyamuni is said to have uttered after his awakening. Literally it means, 'just as comes, just as goes' and connotes the state of perfection. Everything just as it comes and goes is pure and undefiled. Whatever the phenomenal limitation, the Essential is without blemish.

It is with considerable dissatisfaction that I use a word like 'perfect' because it is usually judgmental and dichotomizing, in the sense that it presupposes its opposite, 'imperfect'. Zen has to do with the world of non-duality, which transcends both perfect and imperfect. Perhaps for Christians this is not abstruse, because we refer to God as good and perfect with no possible connotation of the opposite. In any case, the world of the empty-Infinite vivifies all of creation and there are several exclamations frequently lauding this reality, heard in Zen halls: 'The radiance permeates the whole universe.'

When the eminent theologian Catalino Arevalo SJ spoke at the formal installation of our Manila Zen Center in November 1976, his opening sentences were: 'Today is the Feast of Christ the King. Every particle of creation is filled with the beauty of Christ, the love of Christ, the truth of Christ, and the goodness of Christ.' I couldn't help but think any Buddhist I know would applaud that statement.

Teilhard de Chardin is saying the same thing in his *Hymn of the Universe*: 'Maker of the Universe, teach me to adore it by seeing you hidden within. Say once again to me Lord, those great and liberating words, that are at once revealing light and effective poem – *Hoc est corpus meum* – this is my body.'[4]

In Buddhist temples, one frequently sees a statue of Shakyamuni emerging from his experience and reaching down as though to touch the earth. This signifies his desire to return to the phenomenal world where he could help people come to terms with their suffering. As the result of the experience, he was compelled to go out to people and help them shed the shackles keeping them bound, which he found to be the cause of suffering. Shakyamuni subsequently spent the rest of his life in this kind of service to people.

And that is what Zen is all about. Experiencing Tathagata of the universe and then responding appropriately to our world and its violence, injustice, poverty and pollution. Shakyamuni did not just sit. His experience seemed to propel him into action for others. Yamada Roshi used to say if you cannot sympathize with another, there is no satori. Experience realizes itself in involvement. Having found peace, we give peace in service.

At the turn of the decade, I heard a Jesuit specialist analysing the community's efforts during the last decade in being agents of social change. He admitted that on the whole, the programme had failed. An analysis pointed to the fact that change requires process, and personal transformation has to happen before a person can effect change for the better. Social justice and sustainable development cannot happen only on the intellectual level or by an act of the will. They must evolve from a deeper space.

So when we step into the *zendo*, we are determined to reach that space. We leave all our learning and accomplishments as well as troubles and worries at the door. We put ourselves humbly but confidently and with great personal determination in the hands of a qualified teacher. Gradually, we experience the unifying process of Zen practice, and the benefits that accrue from it.

And then as Yamada Roshi used to say, when all things are ready, perhaps at a time least expected, you will break through the barrier and 'shake the earth and astonish the heavens'. You will find that heaven is not beyond the clouds at all, and God is closer than you are to yourself. Or in the words of Zen master Hakuin: 'This very place is the Lotus Land, this very body the Buddha.' You will discover through personal experience that contemplation is indeed the hidden pearl of great price. I urge you to be most faithful to your daily sitting. One day, it will pay joyful dividends.

CHAPTER THREE

Breathing the Spirit

In the preceding chapter, we considered contemporary Christianity and its encounter with Buddhism. We glanced at the Vedic and Dravidic roots of *zazen*, and the beginning of Buddhism, by considering the life of Siddhartha Gautama, better known in the Orient as Shakyamuni Buddha. Now we look at other ancient roots, as we consider the Bible and its meaning of 'person' and 'creation'.

Although gradually being released from its bonds, the Judeo-Christian religion was for centuries frozen in Greek thought patterns, seeing people as an inferior body encompassing a superior soul. Now we are witnessing a revival of the ancient Biblical and Hebraic philosophy. This should help us understand contemporary people better, and also provide a reason for the phenomenon of the great numbers of Christians who are today turning to Oriental prayer methods and feeling they have come home.

The biblical person is seen as a unity, which can be viewed from three different aspects: in Hebrew they are, *bashar* (flesh) related to earth; *nephesh* (soul) orientated to fellow beings; and *ruah* (breath of God) radically focused in God. 'Yahweh God fashioned man of dust from the soil. Then he breathed into his nostrils a breath of life, and thus man became a living being' (Genesis 2:7).

According to Dom Wulstan OSB, 'a person is seen in the

Bible as created for union, by a likeness to God that seeks union with like, *with the breath of God within him acting as a link between them*.[5]

This breathing-God was not unknown to John of the Cross (1542–81). Stanza 39 of his *Spiritual Canticle* speaks of this aspect of God in beautiful medieval phraseology:

The breathing of the air is properly of the Holy Spirit, for which the soul here prays so that she may love God perfectly. She calls it the breathing of the air because it is a most delicate touch and feeling of love which habitually in this state is caused in the soul by the communion of the Holy Spirit. Breathing with His Divine Breath, He raises the soul most sublimely, and informs her that she may breathe in God the same breath of love that the Father breathes in the Son, and the Son in the Father, which is the same Holy Spirit that they breathe into her in the said transformation. And this is for the soul so high a glory, and so profound a delight, that it cannot be described by mortal tongue, nor can human understanding as such, attain to any conception of it.[6]

In a more modern note, a missioner, a contemporary of mine in Japan, Thomas Woodward, says in our phraseology:

I think Eastern religions are onto something when they link prayer to the simple act of breathing, filling our lungs with the ruah, the Spirit of God, breathing the cosmic rhythm. The pneuma, the ruah of God, breathing right into our bodies, filling our lungs, making us live-spirited. How important it is to remember that an incredible power is surging up from the heart of the universe sweeping through the world like the wind, the Spirit of God. To be in touch with that power is always to have enough courage to deal creatively with the world around us.

If there is a shred of truth in all this, how did we ever get so sidetracked as to put our prayerful encounters with the Infinite so predominantly in the intellect? On the one hand, it is amazing that there is so little in classic and modern Christian literature about this other aspect of spirituality. Short phrases in the writings of the early Fathers lead us to believe that they practised a like kind of prayer, but the extracts are snippets only.

On the other hand, it is quite evident that the complementary gift of Christianity to this evolving universal spirituality, is our relationship to the transcendental God. A relationship that implies 'the other'. It is in realization of this that I point out the difference between Western and Oriental meditation.

Along with our religious heritage, there are also the cultural reasons why we overuse the intellect. This is well handled in John Daishin Buksbazen's book *To Forget the Self*:

From infancy onwards, we are very strongly conditioned and taught to rely almost totally upon discursive logic and rational thought. We are generally discouraged from developing or relying on our innate ability to grasp reality intuitively or directly. Such abilities are labelled unscientific and dismissed as weird or even nonexistent. Even when dealing with questions of ultimate reality, we are urged to remain in the modes of thought learned in elementary school classes, and not to entrust ourselves to other ways of knowing reality.

It isn't so terrible to think logically and analytically, if we are designing a bridge or balancing a chequebook. That's the best way to think and be. But when you get right down to it, discursive linear thinking is only useful for certain kinds of tasks, and for others it is quite useless. Like the hammer or the toothbrush, it is a tool intended for certain kinds of jobs. If you use a hammer to brush your teeth, or a toothbrush to drive nails, you are not likely to meet with success.[7]

In his writings and teaching, Anthony de Mello frequently stated that the head is just not a good place for prayer. And certainly the intellect is not a tool for contemplation. Neither are the emotions, imagination, memory nor other faculties of the psyche. They may be creatively used in relational prayer. But for the prayer of communion or identification as Paul de Jaegher calls it[8] they are quite useless. Contemplation leads to an experience, the means of which are not accessible to the human psyche.

The Japanese word *kokoro* is usually translated as 'mind' which unfortunately in English often refers only to the intellect. In Zen it has the wider meaning of consciousness, and when we say 'silence the mind to harmony' we mean that we silence all our spiritual faculties such as the memory, imagination, feelings, as well as the intellect.

In our practice of *zazen* we silence the body by a specified posture and silence the mind by breath-awareness. When we leave our cushions, we do not abandon our zen. What we do away from the cushion is called by the Buddhists 'awareness of being'. In *The Little Manual* given to all novices in a Buddhist monastery, we read:

I remember a short conversation between the Buddha and a philosopher of his time. The philosopher asked, 'I have heard you tell of Buddhism as a doctrine of enlightenment. What is the method? In other words, what do you do every day?' Shakyamuni replied, 'We talk, wash ourselves, sit down . . .' The philosopher broke in, 'What is there that is special in these actions? Everyone talks, eats, bathes, sits down . . .' Shakyamuni said, 'Sir, there is a difference. When we talk, we are aware of the fact that we talk, and so on. When others talk, eat, bathe, or sit down, they are not aware of what they do.'

Could Isaiah perhaps not be saying the same thing? 'Pay attention, come to me; listen and your soul will live' (Isaiah 55:3). It
seems to suggest a certain alertness. In any case, the conversation between Shakyamuni and the philosopher expresses clearly the fundamentality of awareness of being and *The Little
Manual* teaches that it not only produces the power of concentration (absorption is often considered a better English word)
but also gradually sheds light on our daily life style.

Deeper aspects of awareness will be considered later. At this
point, I would like to introduce two other indispensable components of Zen: the teacher and the community of disciples.
Right from the beginning, some acknowledgement has to be
given to the fact that there are very few true Zen teachers in the
world today and it is preferable for a beginner to sit according
to a book, rather than not at all. Be that as it may, it is still an
incontestable fact that once along the Way, one cannot do real
Zen without a true teacher.

In all the Ways of the Orient, a deep bond develops between
the master and disciple, and in Zen we even refer to our teacher
in familial terms, such as 'my father/mother in the dharma'.
On the inside cover of each Kamakura Zendo magazine *Kyosho*
(The Awakening Bell), there is a quotation from Dogen Zenji:

> It should be known that the subtle Dharma of the Seven Bud-
> dhas is maintained with its true significance when it is rightly
> transmitted to an enlightened disciple following an enlightened
> master. This is beyond the knowing of the priest of letter and
> learning.

It is a living transmission, and when something living is transmitted, it is therefore not a doctrine or philosophy. It could
however be said to have four characteristics:

1. Not relying on words or letters.
2. A direct and living transmission outside scriptures.
3. Pointing directly to the mind.
4. The key, is to see into one's True Nature, which is to become an enlightened person.

Where is the starting point? After his great enlightenment, Shakyamuni spent the rest of his life, almost 50 years, teaching and guiding his disciples to realization. Buddhist scriptures recount only one disciple becoming fully enlightened, a certain Kasyapa. To him, Shakyamuni transmitted the 'lamp of the Dharma'. When truly enlightened teachers bring their disciples to an experience congruent with their own, and if the disciples demonstrate teaching ability, they are usually appointed Dharma successors. Following a period of seasoning, in Japan, the honorific title of *Roshi* (literally 'old teacher') is usually bestowed.

When a *roshi* and disciples who want to learn come together in practice, the group is called a *sangha* (Sanskrit for 'community' connoting a kind of alive oneness). As in the master-disciple relationship, the interaction amongst *sangha* members is of great significance. In Zen spirituality, *sangha* is not a noun, but a verb!

Perhaps it would be well for a moment here to consider the Christian parallel. Have you ever wondered what Christ meant when he said, 'for where two or three meet in my name, I shall be there with them'? (Matthew 18:19). Of course we know that Divine Providence is always with us, whether we are alone or with others. It seems that Christ is saying that something extra is added, something special happens, when people pray together. Father de Mello always used to say that contemplation is practised more fruitfully in a group than by oneself.

All sitters agree spontaneously that it is much easier to sit with a group. I suppose part of the explanation is the kind of experience we have all had, of doing something with someone who does it well. A friend tells me that the eminent Canadian theologian Bernard Lonergan claimed this is 'method' in its purest form. For instance, how easy and even thrilling to sing between two vocalists! One is literally carried along and a special relatedness can evoke a bond between the two accompanists.

Something similar happens when we sit together in the dojo (place of practice). It is not uncommon in the Orient for a master to bring a struggling disciple to sit on the next cushion. If the unifying dynamism of *zazen* helps the individual to break down the sense of dualism and separateness, how much more easily will this be generated when there is an added dimension of two or more people, who sit rather deeply in absorption. And one day, the interconnectedness grows to be mutually enriching.

Christianity in both its religion and spirituality has a strong tradition of relationships. Biblical scholars tell us Yahweh is an active verb. God's presence *is* life itself. It's not that the unifying dynamism comes and goes in its life-ing qualities. Hakuin Zenji's *Zazen Wasan* (Song of Zazen) tells us there is, for our Original Nature, no coming or going, and yet it is by always moving to and fro that one is always still. Vibrations are very real to a person sensitized by long hours of *zazen*. Sitting with others, whether more experienced than we are or not, is not only normally supportive, it could be the cause of our own growth and eventual realization.

And when we leave our cushion each day, this generating power continues to move us in compassion and action. Zen spirituality is not just sitting. If we are plugged in, as it were, to the Source of power, we should be shot off our cushions for service in this world of greed, anger and ignorance. Thomas Aquinas says that the best of all lives is when activity flows from a superabundance of contemplation. The personal liberation that comes about through the emptying of oneself, one's selfishness and ego-centred orientation, is not the work of a moment, a few hours of sitting, or months, or even years. In Christian terms it is a work of grace, towards which we dispose ourselves in the practice of sitting, regulating our breathing, and attaining a point of focus.

Once beginners are over the first three or four months, they are usually aware that something is happening, no matter how fragile or tentative at first. If this were not so, then we would have no Zen. It is too difficult a discipline in which to persevere, were there no dividends. The word I like to use in describing the process is 'harmonizing'. In sitting, this happens not only to the individual but to the group as well. This gift of community is best appreciated in fidelity and gratitude. Yamada Roshi would often stand among us in the Kamakura zendo, tasting that dynamism which bonds us. He would warn us not to be unmindful of it.

The term *sangha* may not be of sufficient importance to be retained in our vocabulary, but the fact and happening of community should. As we have said before, a praying community is not a noun but an active verb, and what transpires among the members, creates a bond which is deeply and dearly cherished in an Oriental dojo. The minute we cross its threshold, we renew our awareness of the flow of this sacred unity by the recognition of the Unifier among us, which we do by holding our hands, palm to palm before the face in *gassho* (bow). We next proceed to our cushion, bow to our neighbours, bow again to the whole assembly, and then sit and join in the one-ing.

For your daily practice during the next fortnight, we ask you to change slightly the breath-counting. Continue counting each inhalation, but just watch the exhalation silently, or follow the out-flowing air as you breathe.

CHAPTER FOUR

Practice, Awareness, Zen's Journeying

I n the previous chapter we looked at our own Christian roots by considering the biblical philosophy of person and the breath of God, which is our radical orientation to the Infinite. We saw being alert and breath-centred as an excellent means of reaching the deeper state of consciousness necessary for contemplation. It also led us to consider why we have such a strong propensity to overuse the intellect. The other Zen aspects touched on were the role of the *roshi*, transmission and the *sangha* or community of sitters.

When you sit at home alone, do not neglect to concentrate on your practice. It is considered ideal by most people to sit in the morning as soon as one awakens, the rationale being that the intellect is at that time somewhat still, and is therefore in a helpful state for *zazen*.

If the body and mind are not too exhausted before retiring in the evening, it is also beneficial to sit again at that time. Since sitting helps to quiet the psyche, sleep will be less dream-filled and more restful. However, many people have developed personal habits which make them day people or night people, and sitting times are perhaps best adjusted to these habits. Always sit two or three feet from a wall or curtain, and although keeping the eyes open, do not actually try to focus on seeing any one object.

Yamada Roshi succeeded admirably in maintaining his little

zendo as a sacred place. Perhaps it would be more accurate to say he succeeded in getting his disciples to regard and keep it sacred. As Teilhard de Chardin tells us, there is no place that is secular for those who have the opened eye. This is not a facetious play on words. When Teilhard and Zen masters and the Bible speak about finally seeing with the opened eye, they all mean the same thing. We often refer to this in the Orient as the Third Eye.

In any case do your *zazen* in a place set aside for sitting, an area clean and tidy and away from jarring noises, particularly those of the human voice. Natural sounds like birds or running water or the ticking of a clock can be very helpful for *zazen*. Well I remember the Roshi's assistant, settling us down early one day in *sesshin* with the words, '*Saiwai ni, ame ga futte imasu.*' (You are blessed, it is raining.)

Gassho and bowing and incense and flowers help too. They not only convey a sense of the hallowed, but also tend to keep our senses open. Do not forget clean and comfortable clothing. Zendo regulations call for inconspicuous non-figured clothes with a high neckline. If possible subdued lighting and coolish temperature are desirable.

Despite many stories to the contrary, Zen is not asceticism. There is certainly no coddling in a good *zendo*, but a wise master is not unmindful of the harmful effects of Shakyamuni's excessive asceticism. I remember when I was given permission to make a kind of private *sesshin* under the severe leadership of Fukagai Roshi at Enkoji. She indicated I was to have a little cottage on the temple grounds to myself, gave me the proposed schedule, and then thrust a bag of cookies in my hand, saying, 'Here in case you get hungry. We might forget at times to leave your meal on the doorstep, and you can't sit on an empty stomach.'

As instructed, try to manage one of the prescribed leg positions, preferably the half-lotus, as soon as possible, and sit regularly each day at the same time. Whether you realize it or not, you are developing another habit. If at this point you can sit still for only ten minutes then do ten minutes. Follow that with a five-minute *kinhin*, and then another ten-minute sit, and so on, until you have used up the required sitting time. You may sit as long as your legs will allow, but follow the pattern which *kinhin* sets up. At this point, never sit beyond 25 minutes without leg-relief. This is the rhythm we use in the dojo. Remember the work of *zazen* on the cushion is to forget yourself and become one with your practice. You may still be a little self-conscious, but in time you will become like a veteran driver who simply hops in the car and becomes one with it.

Zazen is very simple really. It is nothing sophisticated or esoteric, as some would have you believe. It is not even very interesting, but the daily feedback and the determination built up to attain your goal will bolster perseverance. Perhaps you are already amazed at the discipline in breath-counting. It is both simple and difficult, a simplicity that admits of no variety, no excitement, no thought content with which to keep your mind entertained.

I spoke about the place of your practice being clean and neat. As we proceed with our *zazen*, we should endeavour to live that way too. A schedule keeps our lives tidy. We should not only organize our work, but also do it in a state of awareness, experiencing at all times. This is practising Zen.

In *The Little Manual* mentioned earlier we read:

In the monastery, the practitioner does everything; he carries water, he looks for firewood, prepares food, cultivates the garden, etc. Although he learns the way to sit in the Zen position, and to practise concentration and meditation in this position, he must strive to remain constantly aware of being, even when he carries water, cooks or cultivates the garden. He knows that to

33

carry water is not only a useful action, it is also to practise Zen. If one does not know how to practise Zen while carrying water, it is useless to live in a monastery.

The practice of awareness of being may seem somewhat artificial in the beginning, but gradually one comes to live in the present moment and at the present place, in a natural way. When we wash the dishes, we just wash dishes – not to get them done – but just to wash dishes. Just standing up, just sitting down, just drinking tea are all practices. I never cease to be amazed that some people devour an entire meal and never seem to taste anything – at least they never comment on the food they are eating. Luncheon business meetings are the bane of Oriental spirituality, as well as the arch-enemy to healthy eating habits. What an unpalatable menu they present to a sensitized palate!

And to live in awareness is to do only one thing at a time. How fractured we become when we do two or three things simultaneously. I recall I used to iron, listen to the radio, and plan the following week's work all at the same time. It never dawned on me why I never liked ironing and why I was such a poor ironer!

When touching on this point of awareness in *teisho* (zen talk), Yamada Roshi would sometimes point to Larry McGarrell, a Jesuit pianist and disciple. 'Have you ever noticed how he gathers all his forces into unity when he plays the piano? As he leans over the keyboard, his whole being is directed towards the music, his body, his mind, his emotions, his everything. If only all that united concentration were directed inwardly, it would be perfect *zazen*.'

Let's check ourselves occasionally and see how aware we are during the day. Not *how* we are doing something, but just the fact that we *are* doing it, the living fact!

The Little Manual continues:

> The practitioner seemingly does exactly the same things as those who do not practise the Way. If, for example, the student shuts the door in a noisy way, he thus proves that he is not aware of his being. Virtue does not consist in the fact of closing the door gently, but in awareness of the fact that one is in the process of closing the door. In this case, the master simply summons his student and reminds him that he must close the door and be mindful of it. He does this, not only in order that the silence of the monastery is to be respected, but also to show the Way of Zen.

And so, away from our cushion, Zen spirituality is correcting wandering thoughts, and this discipline gradually makes us alive to the moment, and being where we are. Ours is a spirituality of very ordinary everyday life. How mighty, clean and pure it is to just sit, just walk, just eat. This is, in Oriental spirituality, to be alive.

What a delight to find in St Paul a hint of a parallel. In 1 Corinthians 10:31, Paul tells us that everything we do is for the glory of God, and when he gives a couple of examples, he does not mention praying, freeing prisoners, or visiting the sick, or even social justice, although these obviously are appropriate venues for the marketplace. He mentions eating and drinking.

As stated above, the here and now is our place and time of practice. It is all we *really* have. In the Zen experience, the Buddha learned that this is not depletion, but a participation in fullness which is 'not yet'. And in this reality all is present, in both past and future.

Zen orientation would have us mindful that we never sit alone. The whole family of creation sits with us. Isaiah pictures the serene reality, (11:6–9)

The wolf lives with the lamb,
the panther lies down with the kid,
calf and lion cub feed together
with a little boy to lead them.
The cow and the bear make friends,
their young lie down together.
The lion eats straw like the ox.
The infant plays over the cobra hole;
into the viper's lair
the young child puts his hand.
They do no hurt, no harm
on all my holy mountain,
for the earth will be full of the knowledge of the Lord
   as the waters swell the sea.

What a reminder of the potential of the ecological reality.

When I left Japan in 1976 with the prospect of sitting alone for an indefinite period, Yamada Roshi wrote a farewell message in his own magnificent calligraphy: *Za ga aru toki, tsune ni, waga iru.* (Whenever you sit, without fail, I will be sitting with you.)

In Japanese Zen orientation, we are asked not to be unaware of the fact that we sit with the great line of fully enlightened Buddhas of all the ages, and all the Bodhisattvas, and Patriarchs. This is a *fact*, not just a religious aspiration.

A Buddha is one who has awakened to the experience of knowing one's True Self. In the West, the word Buddha usually refers to Shakyamuni, the founder of Buddhism, but to the Oriental, it is a more general term and indeed Buddhist scriptures recount legions of Buddhas. Yamada Roshi seemed to feel that we Christians are perhaps inclined to read more than Buddhists do into the man Shakyamuni. 'He was a magnanimous human being and a great teacher who had completed his personality. That is all,' the Roshi used to say.

Bodhisattvas are those delightful people who, though enlightened, only stand at the gate of Nirvana to assist others. One of the most popular in Japan is Jizo, whose replica in stone can be seen in many gardens. Very near the Kamakura Zendo is a busy corner with six of these statues, each sporting a red cap and apron, and two long pockets in the sleeves where Jizo puts small children as he carries them across the busy street.

Patriarchs are the great masters who received and formally transmitted the lamp of the Buddha's illumination, the most famous of whom is Bodhidharma, the first Buddhist missioner who brought Zen from India to China. There are several portraits of the first Patriarch, and all of them portray a great spirit. In biography, it is almost impossible to separate fact from fiction, but it is commonly recounted that he sat alone for nine years before his first disciple, Eka, appeared.

I am reminded of a rather humorous incident which transpired one evening just before I left Japan. I was having supper with the Yamadas, and the Roshi's wife and I were chatting. Several times she exclaimed something to the effect that I would be the first to go and live in the Philippines to teach Zen. 'You'll be just like Bodhidharma,' she exclaimed. Remembering his first nine years of sitting alone, I said, 'I wonder how long it will be before Eka comes.' At this, the Roshi drew himself up to his full stature and looked at me gravely. 'I don't think your concern is about Eka, but whether or not Bodhidharma will be there!'

Probably the words Buddha, Bodhisattva and Patriarch are somewhat familiar and in Zen practice you will meet many of these interesting characters. I guarantee you will enjoy their presence and it seems that not one witless bore survived enlightenment. You will enjoy making friends with these old worthies.

Buddhas and Bodhisattvas and Patriarchs have kept the

lamp burning from Shakyamuni Bodhidharma right down to our day. By the year 1000, there were many Japanese Buddhist monks making the then perilous journey to China to study at the feet of the famous masters there. Great names come to mind such as Dogen Zenji, whom Thomas Merton called his kindred spirit. Dogen brought *Soto* Zen back to Japan and his name and presence is revered in all the Sanbo Kyodan *zendos*.

Indian Zen is considered to have been philosophical. Zen's journey (in the 5th or 6th century AD) into the earthy and poetic hands of the Chinese certainly changed considerably in its encounter with Taoism and Confucianism. Its transfer to Japan saw fewer changes because the Japanese, with their innate sense of excellence, were loath to tamper with this precious jewel. They did, however, give of their own genius and Zen took on new life and vigour in the hands of the pragmatic Japanese.

Now in this twentieth century, Zen continues its journey into different cultures and religions. In North America, this was started by two great teachers, Shibayama Zenkei Roshi and Yasutani Hakuun Roshi. In the early sixties, when I first became interested in studying Zen, Father Hugo Enomiya-Lassalle guided me to the *Rinzai* nuns where I met Tadama Kodo San. She took me to their principal dojo, Enkoji, in north Kyoto, where Fukagai Roshi taught. Its male counterpart is the famous Nanzenji, where Shibayama Roshi was teaching at the time. It was Fukagai Roshi's custom not to give *teisho* during *sesshin*. Instead, we all walked daily to Nanzenji to hear Shibayama Roshi.

I never felt at home in the *Rinzai* harshness of Enkoji, but the thrusts in Shibayama's fine *teisho* were the catalysts I needed to stay, and account for the long period of time I spent in *Rinzai* Zen. Shibayama Roshi journeyed to the United States pointing to the gateless gate, but his successors are caught up in the busy-ness of running Nanzenji and have no apparent overseas apostolate.

Yasutani Roshi, in the *Soto*-based Sanbo Kyodan, made several trips to North America and Europe. He died in March 1973, leaving Yamada Koun Roshi as his chief successor. Into this man's capable hands fell the actual foundation and building of Zen centres in so many other cultures and religions.

At about the same time Japanese Zen moved outward, a momentous thing was happening in Christendom. The Catholic Church in the mid-sixties, under the aegis of the beloved Pope John XXIII, embarked on a renewal which assembled all the bishops throughout the world in the Vatican II Council. Of interest to us here is its document *Ad Gentes* (to the Gentiles) which told Christians and the world that we hold in deep respect all the great religions, for they contain 'those seeds which God's own hand has planted in our ancient cultures even before the Gospel was preached to our people'. In another document, it spoke about different rays of truth that God has entrusted to each of the great religions for which we must search if we are to know the full grandeur of the Infinite.

Vatican II's message was reiterated with even more clarity in the Asian Bishops' Second Plenary Assembly, held in Bangalore, India, in 1978. In their message, the Asian bishops stated:

We are daily more convinced that the Spirit is leading us in our time, not to some dubious syncretism (which we all rightly reject) but to an integration, profound and organic in character, of all that is best in our Asian and traditional forms of prayer and worship, into the treasury of our Christian heritage. Thus is a fuller catholicity made possible in this age of the Church.

We have already dwelt on what Christian prayer has to give Asia. But Asian prayer has much also to offer to authentic

Christian spirituality; a richly-developed prayer of the whole person, in unity of body-psyche-spirit; contemplation of deep interiority and immanence; venerable books and writings; traditions of asceticism and renunciation; techniques of contemplation found in the ancient Eastern religions; simplified prayer forms and other popular expressions of faith and piety.

There are other self-explanatory sections from this amazing document:

The (Asian) Church seeks to share in whatever truly belongs to the culture of our people . . . and this involves a living dialogue with the great religions of Buddhism, Hinduism and Islam . . . over many centuries, they have been a treasury of many of the religious experiences of our ancestors from which our contemporaries do not cease to draw light and strength.

The best means to assimilate the riches of Eastern religious values, and one of the most important ways to contemplation, are in the traditions of ashrams. This will be a specific contribution of Asia to the treasury of the life of humanity at this stage in the growth of the Church.

The techniques developed in Asian religious traditions, such as yoga and zen, are of great service to the prayer experience of immanence. The spirituality of immanence can lead us to newer insights into theology. It can further help us discover an Asian spirituality for Christians.

The real encounter between the Church and our ancient religious traditions will take place at the deeper level of contemplative experiences. Hence the need for the inculturation of prayer of Asian Christians, in keeping with the economy of incarnation which is the law of the Church's life and mission.[9]

Present-day realities in the inter-religious dialogue continue in much the same trend. It would be too extensive an endeavour here to list the interaction among all the different religions, but I should like to mention the visiting exchange now taking place between Tibetan nuns and monks and their American and European counterparts which has caught the eye and heart of all the missionary world.

With my transfer to the Philippines in 1976, Yamada Roshi approved the opening of the Manila Zen Center and one month after arriving in Manila, I was asked by the country's leading theologian to start a Zen Centre for the Filipino Church. When people ask me about the factors involved in placing Zen in the hands of Christians, I not only relate the above, but also exclaim enthusiastically the name of my revered teacher, Yamada Koun Roshi. The moment he welcomed new disciples who were Christian, the Roshi made it clear that he would help them become better Christians. This transpires, not only in the process that sitting is, but also in the Zen experience of *kensho*, to which this great man brought many of his Christian disciples.

Yamada Koun Roshi was freed to do this by the depth of his own experience. He had several sisters, priests, seminarians and committed lay Christians among his disciples, to whom he brought new appreciation of their Christian faith. As he explained many times, he would not have it otherwise. He did wonder why so many Christians came to him for guidance in prayer, and chided those of us whom he allowed to teach, to give the Church a shot in the arm, as far as contemplative prayer is concerned. But he had the highest regard for the Church. He was convinced that the lamp of illumination, the transmission in the line of the great Buddhas and Bodhisattvas and Patriarchs, is the transmission of the true experience of enlightenment. He felt it could be absorbed by all the world's great religions. 'How you articulate that experience within the framework of your own religion is your responsibility,' he used to tell us.

During these years, the Roshi himself grew in appreciation of Christianity, and he often referred to that giant of a missionary, Fr Hugo Enomiya-Lassalle SJ as his ideal human being. And conversely, in a private chat I had with Fr Lassalle one day, he predicted that Yamada Roshi would one day be recognized as one of the greatest Zen masters of our age, because of the gigantic bridge he started building between Buddhist Zen and the rest of the world.

These two leaders died within months of each other, and at a memorial service for Fr Lassalle held in the Tokyo Cathedral, Mrs Yamada was invited to speak. She vividly recounted the intimate relationship that had developed between her husband and the famous Jesuit. She ended by saying, 'I'm sure they're together somewhere right now, discussing the points of convergence between Zen and Christianity.' Let us hope the day will soon dawn when the same relationship can be said to exist amongst the peoples of all religions. Since practising Zen breaks down the sense of supposed separation between the self and others, it is superlative material for the bridge needed in inter-religious dialogue.

CHAPTER FIVE

Sitting Phenomena, Joriki

I n the previous chapter we returned to the cushions, seeing our meditation as an extension of the work we have just left and to which we will be returning. The essential underlying unity has its counterpart in our practice, in the aspect of a constant awareness. We became aware of the fact that we do not sit alone but as one who has embraced all of life, the whole family of creation, from a minute micro-organism to the most advanced human being. We mentioned the effects of the power that is generated in that absorption process, and today we will name and examine it further.

But first, let us return to our cushion and look at something which has probably been an irritant during sitting. Beginners very soon get crowded off the cushion by what we call linear thinking. It often develops into a complete scenario, with people and comments appearing and disappearing on the screen of the mind. When you become aware of this serial, put it aside gently, and return to your breath-counting. Generally speaking, linear thinking seems to bother beginners more than seasoned sitters. When you catch yourself, return 'home' and be firm in determining not to visit the past or future while sitting. The *zafu* is for *zazen* and the present moment only.

After deepening to a certain extent, the bouts of linear thinking become fewer. However, we are often bothered by a solitary mental projection, which is referred to as a random thought. At such a time, we have probably lost the breath-count and an idea pops up on the screen of the mind. We soon become aware of the intruder, and after acknowledging its presence, put it aside gently and resume breath-counting. There is something more or less natural about random thoughts. Yamada Roshi used to refer to them as the wisps of cloud that pass before Mount Fuji. They come for a moment, and then pass away. Try not to let them mean more to you than that.

Sleepiness and staleness are two conditions we have to contend with at times. Splashing cold water on the face or doing a few bending exercises at the end of *kinhin* can be extremely helpful. Or perhaps a couple of well-placed contacts with the *kyosaku* would be helpful!

The *kyosaku* (literally, 'encouragement stick') is the three-foot flat stick usually found on the *zendo* altar. It is very often misunderstood in pseudo-zen circles, where gory stories of its use abound. Unfortunately, with the present dearth of legitimate Zen teachers in Japan today, the custodians of the many beautiful *zendos* throughout the countryside, in the absence of a true *roshi*, find the maintenance bills paid by generously using this stick on curious tourists who want a taste of Zen.

The use of the *kyosaku* (also called the *keisaku* 'correction stick') began in China and was intended then to gently arouse a sleepy sitter. A branch of a tree was used, and the rustling sound of dried leaves at the ear of a drowsy sitter was sufficient to ensure a return to waking consciousness. Over the years, the bough gradually solidified and the stick came to be used as a stimulant for the cluster of blood vessels under the muscles at either side of the base of the neck.

In the introduction to his volume of *teisho* on the Mumonkan, *Zen no Shinzui: Mumonkan*, Yasutani Roshi wrote:

The kyosaku is used for several purposes. It is sometimes known as the batsu (corrective stick) when used to stimulate the lazy or sleepy student. It is also known as shobo (reward stick) when it is used to urge on a student who is doing ardent practice, in the sense of 'yes go that way' as means of approval and stimulation for the student. The kyosaku should be used only when the highest position of leadership and responsibility at the training centre has ordered so. The person who administers the kyosaku should do so with the spirit of compassion and sympathy, while the person who receives the kyosaku does so with the spirit of gratitude.[10]

Adachi Roshi, so often our monitor in Kamakura, says that he uses the *kyosaku* now almost exclusively in response to a request. Some sitters find it extremely helpful. Others do not. The extent to which it is used is up to the sitters generally. If we feel the need for the *kyosaku*, we perform a *gassho* when we are aware that the monitor is making the rounds with the stick.

And so with the help of the *kyosaku*, *sangha* members and teacher, our sitting gradually deepens. A delicate refinement and harmony of body and spirit, mind and breath develops and affects us in many beautiful ways. Our long-held biases and blocks start to loosen their grip, and we feel a little of the freedom that is our birthright. The most unpromising people do change. The delicate path to sitting in perfect oneness is a long slow path, and until inner freedom is attained to some degree, there may be certain maladjustments of body and spirit, mind and breath, which produce sensations.

In our concentration, thought waves on the surface of the consciousness are partially calmed, and elements of past experience in the subconscious are liable to surface. These are called *makyo*. Depending on the individual they may be either pleasant or unpleasant, but never good or bad. *Makyo* is always neutral and must be resolutely set aside. It should be reported to the teacher, however, for it gives some indication of how the sitter is progressing.

The *Ryogon Sutra* lists 50 different kinds of *makyo*. Most often they are visual hallucinations, but *makyo* may also involve sound and (rarely) taste and smell. *Makyo* used to be more prevalent in the early, noisy days of Zen practice. When Yasutani Roshi was still alive, his way more or less prevailed. The four monitors would brandish their *kyosaku* as they hollered encouragement, and many participants pressed down on their practice quite audibly. There was frequent *makyo*.

With Yamada Roshi and his successors, the more quiet Zen prevails. The Roshi felt that Shakyamuni's Zen was quiet, as was that of the great teachers Joshu and Dogen. This way fosters a natural ripening, prolonged a bit perhaps, but leading to a harmonizing experience. Quiet Zen seems to bypass *makyo* to a great extent. Towards the end of his life, Yamada Roshi said that probably only 15 per cent of the sitters in his *zendo* experienced *makyo*.

In my own case, whilst still studying with Fukagai Roshi, I had been asked by Fr Enomiya-Lassalle to help with the first English *sesshin* at his *zendo* west of Tokyo, Shinmeikutsu, Cave of Divine Darkness. Being overseer left me a fair amount of time to sit. Within a couple of days, I began to hear a radio. When I complained to the janitor, he assured me there wasn't one in the area. The following day, I noticed the radio played only when I was sitting and not busy in the kitchen or answering the phone.

One afternoon while sitting in the *zendo*, I was drowsy in the heat, and my head must have nodded. In any case, one of the rookie monitors rushed up, and without any indication of his intention, gave me a couple of good solid whacks with the *kyosaku*. Immediately the 'radio' burst into loud majestic musical chords, which seemed to come from a heavenly organ. Its sound filled the entire universe, and lasted for several minutes, then gradually grew less in volume, and within an hour or so disappeared completely. I never heard it again.

I recognized the *makyo* and related it to Fr Lassalle that evening. He advised me to change teachers and train under one whose name was being frequently mentioned in Zen circles, Yamada Koun Roshi. Within a few months a *kensho* was confirmed during *rohatsu sesshin*, the week-long, annual winter retreat, prior to the anniversary of Shakyamuni's enlightenment.

There is a widely held belief that Christianity considers all visions and their proclamations and miracles as authentic manifestations of God. I would like to point out that the Church has always taught that God *can* intervene and communicate with humans. But the Church is very clear that such manifestations are usually for the individual alone and not necessarily a direct experience of God. The same wise old Church has always discouraged this kind of phenomenon, for we have a good history of persecuting our mystics.

The reason for this reticence is that visions can arise solely from the human psyche, and in our phraseology are wholly *makyo*. There is of course a difficult discernment to be made in determining the authenticity of a mystical revelation, and experience has taught that the visual and auditive forms which arise from the ego far outnumber the ones which come from heaven.

St John of the Cross teaches us to ignore them all. In his *Ascent of Mount Carmel* we read:

I say then, that with regard to all these visions and apprehensions and to all forms and species whatsoever, which represent themselves beneath some particular kind of knowledge or image or form, whether they be false and come from the devil, or recognized as true and coming from God, we must not feed upon them, nor must the soul desire to receive them, lest it shall no longer be detached, free, pure and simple, as is required for union. The reason for this is that all these forms have limitations and that the Wisdom of God wherewith we are to be united contains no limit because it is wholly pure and simple, and God comes not with any image or form or kind of intelligence."

To arrive at this point 'with no form or kind of intelligence' requires power. For our part, this power is generated by the sitting itself. Father de Mello calls it revelation, and the revelation which silence brings is not knowledge. Revelation is power, a mysterious power which in Japanese Zen is called *joriki* (*jo* is 'settling' and *riki* is 'power').

Joriki is the power of strength which arises when the mind has been silenced and unified, and brought to one-pointedness in *zazen* and awareness in daily life. It is a dynamic power which, once mobilized, enables us to act more intuitively. Indeed, the ancient masters teach us that even in the most sudden and unexpected situations we can act instantly and appropriately in a situation, without pausing to collect our wits. Under the power and strength of *joriki*, we are no longer totally ruled by passion nor at the mercy of our environment. We thus gain some measure of freedom and equanimity.

In steady sitting, this power builds up, and as it deepens there may be short experiences of entering *samadhi* (Sanskrit) or *zammai* (Japanese), a state deeper than normal consciousness. It is not a common occurrence and usually happens during *sesshin* on the third or fourth day. It is a deep state of absorption wherein the faculties are in abeyance, and only when the sit is over is one aware of the 'empty' and quick passage of time. As I said, it usually happens well into the retreat, and each sit of 25 minutes seems to be just a few minutes. It can also last a few hours, and under its influence one can participate in *kinhin* without surfacing to normal consciousness. It is sometimes described as the time when the practice takes over. This state too should be reported to the *roshi* during the regular visit to the *dokusan* room (where Zen repartee takes place). It indicates deep sitting.

There are interesting experiments in Japan and the United States with sophisticated machines that monitor what transpires in the human body during *zazen*. Electric wires are attached to different points on the body of the sitter, and the monitoring is indicated on a dial, not unlike an ordinary radio dial. I was told that on that particular machine I was studying, the area between the numbers 12 and 22 constituted the peace and creativity area of the brain, and as we watched, the weak impulse of the alpha waves became stronger the longer the person sat.

I have a friend in California working with a group which is experimenting in alpha biofeedback. The waves emanating from the brain are picked up and magnified, and then fed back to the sitter. Hearing one's own alpha waves apparently excites the brain to greater activity in that area. Since alpha waves emanate from the peace area of the brain, one experiences peace-giving and peace-receiving. My friend claims that she and her associates have helped many people with stress problems. As I remember, the members of the group are all psychologists. They are elated and hopeful for even higher goals, such as a *kensho* experience itself. Yamada Roshi's response to all this was rather reserved: 'They've not produced *kensho* yet, and they won't! There is no *kensho* without sore knees!'

Everyone who has tasted the good effects of Zen (and even some who have not) readily credit *zazen* for cures of psychosomatic illnesses. This is true. There are, though, certain mental disorders that are heightened by all the inward concentration necessary in Zen. It is generally conceded by Zen masters that good mental health is a prerequisite in Zen.

Practising Zen is not all one great rising curve. As the Roshi used to say, it is sitting *yurusareta joken (de)*, under the conditions granted one, and with no manipulation. There will be ups and downs, but through them all, a steady conviction that this is the Way for me. There are many small (and big) stepping stones that become very noticeable to a teacher. Little virtues and big ones start appearing as the fruit of sitting. Most Zen masters do not pass out bouquets. They should not have to. Sitting brings its own rewards.

Not long ago, we had a new young couple join us. The wife is the daughter of two of our older members who joined us a couple of years previously. When I asked the young wife why she wanted to learn Zen, she replied: 'My parents changed so much after they started doing *zazen*, both my husband and I decided to see if we could become that happy too.' That is the kind of promotional work we should do for the *zendo*. Let our person rather than words speak for our practice. Let the God who is the essence of us all speak through our enfleshment.

Today we are going to change the practice. Sitting daily for 30 minutes, you are to continue breath-counting and breath-awareness, but reversing the order. Be aware of the inhalations, and count the exhalations. Do not let yourself become tense! Relax! Smile! And enjoy it all.

CHAPTER SIX

Types of Zen and Other Practices

The Kamakura orientation talks mention five types of Zen. These so-called divisions have meaning for the Japanese, but perhaps do not relate directly to us, so they will be mentioned only briefly. The first, *Bompu Zen*, or ordinary Zen, is nothing more than quiet sitting, which is an integral part of Japanese life (or at least it used to be).

The second type is *Gedo Zen*, 'outside the Way Zen', which includes all teachings other than Buddhist.

The third and fourth types are *Shojo* and *Daijo*, which mean literally, the 'small vehicle' and the 'large vehicle'. They point directly to Hinayana (small vehicle) and Mahayana (large vehicle) Buddhism. Hinayana is also Theravada (the Way of the Elders). It might be well for us to use the term too, as it would tend externally at least, to break down the dichotomy inherent in the terms Mahayana and Hinayana.

Generally speaking, Theravada Buddhism spread throughout the south of Asia, in Sri Lanka, Burma, Thailand, Kampuchea and Laos. Several of the Buddhist monasteries in England are Tibetan, but the majority are in the Theravadan tradition. It discourages syncretism and maintains a strict adherence to the basic tenets of Buddhism. Hinayana can perhaps be compared to a bicycle designed to accommodate only one's own self, hence the term 'small vehicle'. In these days of widespread drug abuse and sexual licence, the moralistic basics of Theravada have much to offer young people in the West. Monasteries are being established in many areas, and aspirants take their vows to follow the Buddhist precepts.

Mahayana spread to Tibet, China, Korea and Japan, blended with the cultures it entered, and developed national characteristics. Zen Buddhism as we know it today developed in this tradition in China, and has been preserved for us by the Japanese. There is no moralistic preaching in a *zendo*. Zen teaches that right action arises naturally from the heart, and to impose a moral code as an ideal on an aspirant is to do violence to that person's spiritual life. Of course a good teacher encourages right living, but does so on an individual basis. The large vehicle can be compared to a bus, where all are saved helping one another. But it is interesting to note that many works in social action in Southeast Asia seem to be coming from the Theravada community.

The fifth and last type of Zen is called *Saijojo* (highest vehicle). This is the Zen Dogen Zenji chiefly advocated, and is represented by the practice of *shikantaza* (just sitting). In this highest Way, means and end coalesce.

Shikantaza is not supported by any such aids as breath counting, following the breath, or doing a *koan*. It is therefore very easy for the mind to become distracted in *shikantaza*. It is a type of *zazen* where the mind must be unhurried, yet at the same time firmly planted or massively composed like Mount Fuji. In *shikantaza*, the body 'just sits', the breath 'just sits', the mind 'just sits'. All is manifested right here.

Now, when people ask me about the types of Zen, I am inclined not to mention the five above-mentioned groups but rather the three extant sects in Japan now. (Zen Buddhism is alive in Korea, but its most prominent teacher took his training in Japan. As far as I know there is no Zen in mainland China or India now, and Tibetan monasteries do not give to sitting the same significance as we do.)

Mahayana Buddhism has been the home of *zazen* for centuries in Japan. There are three remaining sects: *Rinzai*, *Soto* and *Obaku*. They are at the crossroads today, if not altogether dying. *Obaku* seems to have settled on promoting Zen food. Its enlarged restaurant in Uji is bigger than its main temple! The *Soto* sect, which Dogen Zenji brought back to Japan, grew and flourished in the Kamakura period, but has been weakening and is now gasping its last breath. *Soto* is called 'farmer Zen', not in the sense of being a country bumpkin, but because each disciple is tended individually as farmers used to treat their many kinds of plants separately and with much care.

Sometimes called 'warrior Zen', *Rinzai* also attained prominence in the Kamakura period and then experienced a decline, but with its Tokugawa spirit, it has earned the name of the Zen of General Rinzai. It is in better shape than *Soto* Zen at the moment, and still has a few truly enlightened *roshis* as teachers. The credit for some of its present healthy state is due to the *koan* system used in its training programme, as well as its rebirth through Hakuin Zenji (1686–1769).

Our stream of Zen, the Sanbo Kyodan, was founded by Harada Sogaku Roshi, born in 1870. Harada Roshi belonged to the *Soto* sect, but not being able to find an adequate teacher therein, he went to a *Rinzai* monastery for training. His subsequent teaching was a combination of the sitting of *Soto* and the *koans* of *Rinzai*. He died in 1961. His successor, Yasutani Roshi, actually legally institutionalized the Sanbo Kyodan, and conducted *sesshin* not only all over Japan but in North America and Europe as well. He died in 1972 and Yamada Koun Roshi, a layman, became his successor. Yamada Roshi, the beloved and revered teacher of so many Japanese and non-Japanese practitioners, passed away peacefully at his home on September 13, 1989. He was succeeded by Kubota Ji-un Roshi.

In discussing *Gedo Zen*, I said I did not consider most forms of Christian prayer to be zenlike. Let's have a short look at some of the popular kinds of prayer being used by Christians today.

Since Vatican II, there has been widespread interest in all kinds of prayer. There is a saying that we should pray as we can, but that does not mean chaos. If there were such a thing as a prayer clinic, it would have a varied pharmacy. There are many methods to suit various needs. We must realize that if we are to take prayer seriously, that does not permit indiscretion. This may sound ridiculous, but I have heard more than once, people saying: 'I do the Jesus Prayer and the Cloud Prayer with a little yoga and Zen thrown in, and I put them all together.' All the great prayer traditions in the world have their own ethos, and should be respected.

Orthodox masters call the Jesus Prayer the Prayer of the Heart. The heart is the seat of human and divine warmth, and many feel an attraction to this prayer. After some experience in dealing with people who experienced problems with it, Tony de Mello said it is not to be undertaken lightly and only under a qualified teacher, or it can be psychologically damaging. For many years, masters in the Jesus Prayer could not be found on Mount Athos in Greece, which used to be its home. I am told they have happily returned, and it is thriving there once again, thus belying the prediction that soon the masters of the Jesus Prayer would be found only in books.

Any number of people tell me they are doing the Jesus Prayer, by which they usually mean short ejaculatory prayers. Good! If you are happy doing your prayer that way, it is excellent. Just do not forget, that too will tend to simplify. Very soon you will have nothing left, and this is an ideal state. But you will need guidance in how to carry on with nothingness. Go to a teacher in non-object or completely silent prayer.

Centring Prayer is the name given to the kind of prayer

Thomas Merton advocated. I am told he apparently used the word 'centring' rather frequently in his discourses on prayer, and the name stuck. It is not new to the twentieth century, but rather has its roots in the old monastic prayer of the Church which goes back seventeen hundred years. Later it became known as the Prayer of the Cloud of Unknowing. Today, there are not only excellent books on the Centring Prayer, but also tapes, and best of all, masters who produce them.

Another form of guidance in prayer may be found in the spiritual tradition of Ignatius of Loyola, presented so ably by the Jesuit Fathers as well as by other priests, sisters and lay people.

The charismatic and *cursillo* experiences seem to be an excellent vehicle for more socially-inclined worshippers, and surely all of us at some time during a week surge forth in charismatic exclamations. There is a time for words in prayer, there is a time for the silence of contemplation. The individual, with the help of a director, can decide on how much time to give to each.

Make no mistake, the way to inner depths through silence takes courage and determination. A deep state of consciousness is a place where healing and experience happen, but to get there we must abandon objects in our contemplation. Here the Oriental Ways are invaluable, because they start with the non-objective stage.

All Oriental meditation is simplicity itself. When asked to speak about its characteristics, I usually list them as:

- Non-objective and directed inward.
- Breath-centred; its matter is not contained in words, ideas, concepts, feeling or imagination.
- Body participation, it involves the whole person.
- A long apprenticeship, a legacy to be received/bequeathed.
- A master-disciple relationship, it cannot be learned through books.

- Use of koans, all things and nothing.
- Experience-orientated.
- Healing and transforming, a discipline.
- Means and end coalesce.

We start with the dictum, pray as you can and allow yourself to be led. This is underlined by Yamada Roshi's response which has meant so much to me over the years. When I asked him what he thought prayer should be for the Christian, he immediately replied, 'It should be the same as prayer for the Buddhist. Prayer is light sitting in light.' In Christian terms, it seems to me that something of this is caught in the word *Abba* (Father).

Following the method we are presenting here now, plus a little courage and Spartan spirit, with the help of grace, we can conquer inner space. Like modern scientists learning the secrets of the moon, we can be led to enter the land of the sun, and find the light and warmth we seek so assiduously.

CHAPTER SEVEN

Aims of Zen

In the last chapter, we considered Christian prayer, the characteristics of Oriental prayer, and finally the five types of Zen. This led to a discussion of our own stream of Zen, the Sanbo Kyodan. Today I would like to start at that point, and explain the meaning of those two words. Sanbo Kyodan literally means 'The Three Treasures Teaching Group'.

The Three Treasures of Buddhism often appear in the sutras. The first treasure is the Buddha, not in the particularized sense of Shakyamuni, but as the ubiquitous empty-Infinite that vivifies all the universe.

The second is the Dharma, a Sanskrit word that is very rich in meaning. The root is the verb *dhr*, which means 'to hold together or support'. As a noun, it means that which makes something what it is, or as we say in modern parlance, its 'is-ness'. Everything in the universe has its own dharma. In actual use, the word has many implications, and frequently implies 'law', the law of the universe which is the way things are. It naturally points to the Buddha's teachings, the principle, the lamp. Robert Aitken Roshi of the Honolulu Zendo sees the Dharma as having to do with things, always in motion, always interacting with other things. And so all phenomena are not nouns, but verbs!

The third treasure is the Sangha, the living community, of which we have spoken so much. We did, however, use the word in the sense of our own group. As one of the Three Treasures, it refers to the fellowship of all things. Saint Francis talking to Sister Moon, as a poet greeting a rose: 'How lovely you are!'

It points to the first of the four vows, recited many times daily in a *zendo*. Since vows have a special place in the Church, we decided in our *zendo* to call them 'aspirations' and our translation is as follows:

Creations are innumerable,
    I resolve to free them all.
Delusions are inexhaustible,
    I resolve to extinguish them all.
The aspects of truth are countless,
    I resolve to learn and master them all.
The way of enlightenment is peerless,
    I resolve to accomplish it.

The Three Treasures are the hearth and home of the Zen student. Although we do not use it, there is a prayer chanted in Buddhist *zendos*: 'We take refuge in the Buddha. We take refuge in the Dharma. We take refuge in the Sangha.' Let us not forget what home implies, loving care and devotion, letting go of the aggressive self to give way to the True Self. Our Zen centre is our physical refuge which has at least one training period (*ango*) annually. But in reality, we try to make every day a training day, and every place a dojo, a training place. To do this we must always keep in mind Yasutani Roshi's warning that the fundamental delusion is our separation from all else. Let us resolve to come to a deep realization that we share a single organism (if what Paul calls Divine Nature can be termed 'organism') with all creation. We learn to apply this to our daily life starting here in our home.

Yamada Roshi emphasized the importance for beginners in Zen to comprehend its aims clearly. What do we attain by doing *zazen*?

He listed three categories:

1. developing concentration of the mind, joriki
2. satori awakening, or enlightenment
3. personalization of satori

Joriki

First, the power of *joriki*, the power which arises from silence, stillness power, which eventually can make all effort on our part, impossible.

Yamada Roshi used to recount that towards the end of Harada Roshi's life, the latest in a long line of Hinayana purists from the South came to exhort his northern brethren. By way of demonstration, he said to monks who had gathered in a Tokyo hotel room that he would go into deep concentration and gradually the chair on which he was sitting would ascend to the ceiling and remain there for 55 minutes. So he started concentrating and, quite surely, chair and monk betook themselves to the ceiling, and only after 55 minutes elapsed did they safely return to the floor. 'Now,' he told the assembled monks, 'I would like to see the state of your concentration.'

Harada Roshi's representative went home crestfallen, telling his teacher: 'I could do nothing.' The Roshi with the traditional vigour of a great Zen master said, 'I wish I had been there. I would have said, my friend you must be tired and thirsty after your trip. I pray you have a cup of tea.' And in characteristic Zen fashion, the Roshi extended his hand as though serving tea. 'Bah!' he exclaimed, 'who was that monk helping up there at the ceiling!'

Yasutani Roshi declared that the fourth type of Zen, *Daijo* or greater vehicle, is the true Buddhist Zen. It is Mahayana Zen, and as a large vehicle, it can be compared to a car, or better yet a bus. It is the Zen of enlightenment, seeing into your Essential Nature and realizing the way in one's daily life.

It is interesting to note here that Mahayana Zen spread mostly to northern countries in Asia, where it fused into the cultures of China, Japan and Korea. It seems that the Zen of Christians will come from Japanese Mahayana. This is more than appropriate. Christians are notorious bus travellers!

Yamada Roshi taught that *joriki*, the ability to concentrate, is of utmost importance in establishing and maintaining a successful life in this world. It calms the surface of our consciousness. This is necessary in making correct decisions and for receiving external impressions and information the right way.

When we want to transfer a message or image from an inked rubber stamp to a piece of paper, we make sure that the paper is empty, smooth and clean. Otherwise the image on the stamp will not print clearly, but will be blurred and difficult to read. If the paper is crumpled it will be entirely unintelligible. Our mind must be empty and smooth if we want to be able to hear what people are really saying to us. I recall asking a person who was upset what she thought of a certain situation, and she answered that I could remain living where I was! The answer had no relation to the question. Her mind was crumpled. Some emptying and *joriki* would have helped to smooth it out.

The mind that is deeply absorbed does not yield easily to the influence of external circumstances. We can eliminate our distractions by sitting. And moreover, when we want to actualize ideas which arise in our heart, or when we want to accomplish some work, strong concentration of mind is indispensable.

When you hear this, does it not strike you that *zazen* is a balm for many of the ills of our society today? From some of my reading, it seems that Carl Jung and Erich Fromm have praised it as a kind of panacea for most of the mental illness plaguing the world today. I am not aware that either of these men had actual Zen training, and if they are speaking only from theory, it's an inadequate base for Zen truth. They were not completely wrong, but a mentally unstable person is no candidate for Zen training. The number of psychotics and neurotics from the West who fled to Japanese *zendos* in the late fifties and early sixties was formidable. It led Yamada Roshi to exclaim at one point that a *zendo* was not a hospital ward. *Zazen* is not for the sick and for certain types of mental illness all its inner concentration can even be harmful.

Whether the Japanese do *zazen* or not, they are not mistaken as to its worth. They see sitting as an intense inner struggle to gain control over their *kokoro*, their heart-mind, the discipline of which winds its way into all facets of life. This has penetrated Japanese thought and culture for a thousand years. In *zazen* is the seat of *joriki*, all else is the Way, the Do, the *Michi*, the Tao of China. Just a few examples are the way of tea (*sado*), the way of flowers (*kado*), the way of writings (*shodo*), the way of archery (*kyudo*), the way of fencing (*kendo*) and the other well-known ways of judo, aikido and so on.

These are all children of Zen. When young Germans or Americans came to the San-un Zendo and told the Roshi they wanted to do *zazen* to help their aikido, he kindly but firmly taught that aikido is a child of Zen, and not the other way around. It is training in the art of directing the flow of *joriki*, the power which arises from the absorbed mind.

I feel that other effects of that power are vividly illustrated in the life of the evangelist St Paul. The whole impetus of his dynamism were acts of power. As a missionary, he always acted with power. His works were explosions of power, and he apparently learned all his doctrine from that great religious experience that exploded into action. Power in prayer, in experience, and in action, these are all contained in the first aim of *zazen*, which is *joriki*.

Satori

The second aim of Zen is *kensho godo*, satori awakening or enlightenment. It is seeing into your true nature and at the same time seeing into the nature of the universe with its 10,000 things. *Tathagata*! I have been complete from the very beginning. How wonderful! A true *kensho* is always the same for whoever experiences it. But the depth of the experience necessarily varies, for in the completeness of the experience, there are great degrees.

Yasutani Roshi always likened the opening of the third eye to a person blind from birth who only gradually begins to recover his sight. At first he sees vaguely and then only nearby things. Later, as sight improves, he is able to distinguish things a yard or so away, then many yards, until finally he can recognize anything up to a thousand yards. At each of these stages, the phenomenal world he is seeing is the same. But there are great differences in his vision at each step. So it is with the difference in clarity and depth of our experiences of *kensho*.

Kensho which literally means 'to see (Essential) Nature' is of utmost importance to a Mahayana Buddhist. Dogen has clearly stated that without enlightenment there is no Zen. This satori does not necessarily happen by mere concentration or absorption. This is especially true when the mind is brought to one-pointedness in the objective world. And even when this is achieved inwardly, our main problem, that of life and death, cannot be solved fundamentally by concentration. It can only be solved by enlightenment and the personalization of that experience. So if we want to free ourselves from the anxiety of the sufferings of life through *zazen*, the satori experience should be our main purpose of practice. Dogen has told us to pray for help in achieving this, which belies the commonly held belief among Buddhists that we can come to satori through our own efforts alone.

For the Buddhist, satori is the gate of salvation. It is utterly indispensable. Now what is this experience for us Christians? We name our Absolute 'God', and *kensho* for us would be seeing into the nature of the indwelling God and the 10,000 creations. We are perhaps not as willing as Buddhists to admit that our number one problem is that of 'life and death'. We have been heavily imbued with the certainty that we are already redeemed, and have only to do the 'part' that is left undone in the salvation of the world. On the other hand, the present popularity of books on 'near death' experiences, is awakening many of us to that journey we will be making some day.

Is the experience of seeing into the ultimate nature of God and the 10,000 creations any less dispensable for us Christians at the close of the twentieth century? Has not our Christianity become irrelevant for a great segment of our people? The wealth and power structures within the Church are anathema to the poor and to women. And the lessening numbers of those who remain faithful to these issues are frighteningly susceptible to frustration, burn-out, and despair.

And where are the helps and guidelines needed at this time of great changes in our paradigm and world view? Certainly not in our religious leaders who are conspicuously either absent or preaching the old-time religion. Many authors analysing the present condition, frequently quote Dostoevsky's Grand Inquisitor. Truly, would we recognize Jesus Christ if he returned today to the marketplace? I think we have lost touch with our God. I think we need to meet again, to recognize and come to know one another, but in the light of what Father

Lassalle said, perhaps on a deeper and more experiential level.

How often the Bible tells us just that, in the lovely words from Hosea with which we begin our sittings: 'I don't want your sacrifices, I want your love. I don't want your offerings, I want you to know me.' And in the simple wisdom of Psalm 46: 'Be still and know that I am God.' In the New Testament too, we have almost countless cases in Paul's letters, as when he prays for the Colossians that they will have a rich experience of *knowing* Christ. That changed Paul's life. It can change ours.

The new paradigm into which we are moving is precisely to bring us to a new dimension of faith in the Ultimate and its 10,000 creations. Father Lassalle says it will be a mystical, intuitive and direct way of knowing, a reflection of the kind of seeing we experience in *kensho*. I like to think that to be led in and through this experience is the ultimate reason for all of us in Zen.

Personalizing Satori

The third aim of *zazen* is *mujudo no taigen* or the personalization of satori. It is the actualization of the Supreme Way throughout our entire being, and our daily activities. At this point we do not distinguish end from means. *Saijojo*, which is the fifth and highest of the five types of Zen, corresponds to this stage. When you sit earnestly and egolessly in accordance with the instruction of a competent teacher, that is with your mind though fully conscious, as free of thought as a pure white sheet of paper is unmarred by a blemish, there is an unfolding of your intrinsic pure Original Nature. Some Chinese texts refer to this unfolding as our Essential Nature returning to its original spontaneity, which teaching, for me, struck an especially deep chord within.

The third aim of *zazen*, the personalization or embodiment of satori, comes as a matter of course, only after having attained the experience. To come to it is not very difficult. For some people, only one *sesshin* is necessary. But to accomplish our ultimate personality is very difficult indeed, and requires a long period of time. The experience itself is only the entrance. The completion is to personalize what we came to realize at the moment of awakening. And then, after washing away all the glitter and ecstasy, the truly great Zen people are not distinguishable in outward appearance. They are people who have experienced deep enlightenment and consequently extinguished all illusion, but are still not different externally from other ordinary human beings. Through *zazen* and *kensho*, you don't become a special person or a strange person, or an eccentric and esoteric character. You become a normal person, a real person, and as far as possible, a true human being. 'I think the truly great Christian is not much different,' the Roshi once remarked.

In his *teisho* at the Kamakura Zendo, the Roshi often referred to throwing away the experience, discarding it completely, and proceeding to the marketplace. He always taught that virtue rises in the heart, and that the wisdom of satori inevitably brings a corresponding impulse to compassion. To us Christians he seemed to be saying, 'We are here living amongst humankind, and not on the top of Mount Tabor.' On this point, Jesus' words as recorded in John, came to mind: 'Now that you know this, happiness will be yours, if you behave accordingly.' After we have come to know, we are compelled to *do*!

Parallel to Christianity and other great religions of the world, Zen Buddhism's history is a record of deeply enlightened monks turning their backs on satori, and labouring tirelessly to meet the needs of the people amongst whom they were living. Lots of *joriki* is needed if one is to persevere, and therefore lots of sitting. It will be no different for any of us when our time comes. If as a Christian you realize through experience that you are indeed another Christ and that all peoples are your brothers and sisters, you will be an effective unifying power in the world. Considering our many problems today, this happening and process is precisely what is needed to restore harmony in the universe, and to make Earth a nourishing home for ourselves and our children.

Our practice for the final two weeks is just sitting. It is difficult and usually used only by mature sitters. We nevertheless suggest it as your present 'work' on the cushion. You just may be very good at it, for we occasionally find a beginner for whom this simplicity is natural. After getting yourself settled on the cushion, count the breath for one or two sequences. Then stop the counting and just follow the breath. Just that. Keep trying.

CHAPTER EIGHT

Koans and Shoken Preparation

There are two facets to the practice for the true practitioner of Zen: *dokusan*, the private interview, and *teisho*, the public teaching, both given by a trained and approved teacher. But before we go into their use, we have to consider *koans* first, because both *dokusan* and *teisho*, in our stream of Zen, have *koans* at their heart.

People all over the world are gradually becoming familiar with the word *koan*. It is sometimes compared (rather inaccurately, I think) to the parables in the gospels. In any case, it was interesting to read a Newsweek article describing parables as having a parallel effect to *koans*!

The first *kanji*, *ko*, is 'public' or 'common to all'. The *an* is usually translated as 'announcement' or 'presentation of the truth'. So a *koan* is a presentation of a truth common to all. Shibayama Roshi says the etymology of the word is 'the place where the truth dwells'. The important point not contained in either definition is that it is usually expressed as a riddle or conundrum, in baffling language which the intellect cannot accept.

If a *koan* is the presentation of a truth common to all expressed in riddle form, the Zen masters could create them on the spot at any time and there could be literally thousands of *koans*. That is probably so. There are also many volumes of recorded *koans* as well, one in *Rinzai* containing over 5000. In the Sanbo Kyodan, we use six volumes, four of which are widely used in training centres. These are:

1. Mumonkan (The Gateless Gate)   96 koans
2. Hekigan roku (The Blue Cliff Record)   100 koans
3. Shoyoroku (The Book of Equanimity)   100 koans
4. Denkoroku (The Transmission of the Light)   100 koans

In the Sanbo Kyodan, we start with a small volume of 24 miscellaneous *koans* which Harada Roshi compiled. And then at the end of our formal study, there is Yasutani Roshi's compilation of some important Zen Buddhist texts, including Tozan's Five Ranks and Dogen's teaching on the Ten Grave Precepts. This is not specifically a *koan* text but some parts are presented as *koans*.

One of the best-known *koans* is *Sekishu*, or The Sound of One Hand. On the surface, it does not make much sense. Two hands can make a sound by clapping, but not one alone. Now of course if you think long enough, you will come up with an answer, which is usually unacceptable because it has been thought out. It is often said that the appropriate answer is intuited. This *koan* is considered difficult and usually not given to beginners.

In the Sanbo Kyodan, the Muji *koan* is given first:

A monk asked Joshu, 'Does a dog have Buddha Nature or not?' Joshu replied, 'Mu.'

This is a very simple and direct *koan*. Joshu was a famous and capable Zen master and is here being tested by one of his monks. The question is intellectual, and the disciple expects the teacher to transcend 'has' and 'has not' whilst not eschewing Joshu's splendid thrust of 'Mu!'

The Master's reply means nothing to the intellect. And the roshi will probe at each *dokusan* into what Mu is. This is a specific *koan*, and the disciple is taught how to grapple with it. As awareness and silence deepen, the sitter gradually becomes more and more absorbed in Mu. *Sesshin* provides the ideal ambience. Absorption will present certain conditions to the consciousness, and then one moment when all things are ready, a reaction will occur which may or may not be *kensho*. It will be examined at *dokusan*. The real experience has been described in various ways such as the universe collapsing or the body and mind falling away. Whatever the particular articulation, it is an experience of a Nothingness that is infinitely potential. And in that Nothingness, there is no possible division. Everything is always one.

In this happening, Mu will reveal itself, and in a true *kensho*, the confidence of the disciple is readily manifest. Also, the questions thrust out by the teacher fall into the orbit of the experience, and an appropriate response is immediate and certain. The experience itself can vary in depth, and a deep experience is accompanied by great joy. When the teacher has certified the experience, the disciple then proceeds with the other *koans*, which widen the area of 'sight', hence the frequent use of the word 'insight'. Gradually, in the light of this wisdom and spurred on by it, we engage in the works in the marketplace of the world, with its greed, anger, injustice, ignorance, pollution, poverty and war.

Speaking of the marketplace, that is where *koans* are born. They take as their subject concrete and everyday objects such as a dog, a fox, a finger, a beard, a tree, a flower. And *koans* have a kind of tactile approach to these subjects to offset our long-nourished necessity to secure them in abstract concepts.

Within this wide range of objects, the *koans* are all pointing to the same Reality, with a lightness that belies their ultimate value. These marvellous creations of the ancient Chinese masters keep teasing the intellect to admit that it has limitations. And when it surrenders with an 'ah' there is a moment of sheer joy and delight. As a Zen student, I found them a most delightful means of learning, and consider them a worthy standard for the spiritual genius of the Orient.

In working on the *koan* Mu, eventually the apparent gap between ourselves and Mu lessens and we suddenly become one with it. In the action of becoming one with something, we break down the illusive barriers that seem to separate us. We soon come to realize that suffering is caused by this illusion, namely separation. There is a way of reading the New Testament writings of Paul to see that there is only one sin, that of separation. In action, we are one with the real situation. The secret is to be or to do and not to think.

I recall teaching English at a steel company in Japan where I was asked what I would exclaim if I knocked over something accidentally. I thought for a moment or two and then gave a reply. The men were apparently not convinced and later simulated an awkward situation and eventually I knocked over a glass of water. Extemporaneously I exclaimed something quite different from the considered reply. A spontaneous response is closer to the centre. In Zen, second thoughts are not always desirable.

A *koan* is not a verbal game. It does incite intuition. Not only the content of the *koan*, but the manner of presentation must be vigorous, spontaneous, and 'one with'. A *koan* is anti-intellectual only in the sense that the intellect cannot bring us to the Zen experience.

In a *zendo*, one frequently hears the Chinese story of the 500 stupid monkeys. Walking along together one night, the first monkey happened to look down a well by the side of the road, and saw the moon. He was very disturbed and called his companions to look. They all shared his dismay that the moon might drown down there in that well and then there would be no light at night. So they resolved to save the moon. The first monkey lowered his body into the well by entwining his arms around a nearby tree. The second monkey climbed down and entwined his arms through the curved tail of the first monkey, and so down through them all. Just as the 500th monkey was climbing down to be the one to save the moon, the tree broke, and they all drowned in the deep dark well of their delusion.

A *koan* attempts to lead us to direct experience. In our training, we do not sit with *koans* in the sense of trying to figure them out while we are sitting. We sit harmonized in body and mind, with whatever our practice is. We deal with *koans* in *dokusan* and *teisho*.

The subject matter of *koans* has to do with ordinary simple everyday things, like dogs and fingers and foxes and bears and trees and flowers. Certain religious people express alarm that these subjects are not overtly religious. Obviously there is for them both the sacred and the secular.

When I glance away from the screen of this word processor, I see a palm tree, which is not Christian, not Buddhist, but just a palm tree. When you read or hear 'palm tree' you have your own internal picture of one. If there are 100 people reading this text, then 100 palm trees will appear, and they will all be different. If I should use the word 'God' in a *teisho* in front of 35 people, I am aware that 35 gods appear on their minds' screen. These are conceptualized gods. Concepts are fine in theory, but they kill *koans*. A tree is a *koan par excellence*, as has been attested by several of our members. In Zen spirituality, the word *secular* is not a reality.

Koan subjects are very concrete and act merely as a momentary catalyst, and are not intended as material for contemplation or intrinsic debate. The Oriental master would remind us that doing and thinking and feeling objectify the world, and put us in the ambience of separation, where the ego is strengthened. And here I give a word of caution to spiritual directors who overuse the multiplying methods suggested in Western psychology which strengthen the ego. If there is a psychological problem then psychotherapy may be indicated, but I have always felt it is a risky business for any healthy person, an Oriental in particular, to be in a process of ego strengthening for an extended period of time. This goes contrary to the basic tenets of Oriental spirituality, their birthright. For an Occidental, there is already a mind-overload, which needs lessening. For them, *zazen* at first is an antidote.

One time, an American priest who professed ignorance of Zen said Mass at the Zen Center, Philippines, and during the homily blurted out, 'I don't know much about Zen, but you know, all you can really do in contemplative prayer is mortification.' He understood Zen better than he thought, although I would have added 'gratitude'. We may not be inclined to call our silencing mortification, but it is. John of the Cross calls it 'the dark night of the soul' and David in the Psalms speaks of 'the valley of the shadow of death'. We do not pretend to understand all of its ramifications, but discipline does bring about a harmony of body and psyche and the unifying dynamism speaks its own language which we can all appreciate.

We use *koans* in the *dokusan* situation. *Doku* means alone, and the *kanji* has the reading of *hitori-deni* which means 'of itself' or 'spontaneously'. *San* is 'to go' or 'to visit'. So *dokusan* is to go see the *roshi* alone and act in a spontaneous manner.

What passes between teacher and disciple in *dokusan* is for the two only. Since it involves *koan* work, the need for privacy is self-evident. As sitting deepens, the teacher prods with a technique called *mondo*, literally 'questions and answers'. It goes without saying that the questions are loaded, and groping for the appropriate response provides a friction which can produce the spark for *kensho*.

It is like the chemicals on the tip of a matchstick. The longer the sitting, the more the chemicals build up. However, if this is the only condition that exists, one can sit for years without coming to light. We need an abrasive, the side of the matchbox, for a light, and this is one of the functions of the teacher. To know the response of a *koan* ahead of time is to put grease on the abrasive.

One of the signs of decadence in Japanese Zen training centres over the past two centuries is the existence of books of answers to *koans*, which come from an oral transmission. When celibacy died in Japanese Buddhism, zen teachers married and had families, and the potent custom of *chonan* (eldest son) inheriting the father's station could not be abandoned. Even if the son knew nothing about *koan* and *satori*, he had to take over his father's position as *roshi*. For a small fee or favour from indigent old-timers, the problem was overcome. So *koans* were robbed of their vigour and very life.

In the intimacy of the *dokusan* room, the wisdom and compassion of a true teacher comes to aid and challenge the disciples. After his death, a poem Yamada Roshi had composed on the occasion of his 77th birthday was made public. It reads:

Once an old buddha said
The mind of bright Wisdom
Is nothing but the mountains, rivers, great earth,
The sun, moon and stars.
One night I realized this: all of a sudden
Heaven and earth collapsed
And were reduced to dust,
Clearly I have seen
Not one thing, no man, no buddha.

My karmic sins were all extinguished
As if in a bolt of lightning.
And what is it after all?
Nothing special: just this, just this.
You see how my eyes are;
They do not talk,
And they look void
Of any anxiety.

> THE 8TH DAY OF THE MONTH OF RO
> IN THE 59TH YEAR OF THE SHOWA ERA
> (8 DECEMBER, 1984).
> KOUN-KEN ZENSHIN
> OLD MAN OF 77 YEARS[12]

Abhishiktananda, in speaking about a sannyasin (holy wanderer) describes a *roshi* as well:

> He will show them in his life how to perform their ordinary human tasks with the fullest consciousness combined with total detachment; and at the same time how to maintain an unswerving attention to the Presence, even in the midst of daily occupations and concerns.[13]

Such is the Way of Zen. At least this has been a theoretical explanation which you can bring to life, if you choose. As said previously, in one sense, Zen is an emptying process, which effects a gradual accompanying sensitizing. It is also complete and replete with perfection at all times and places.

Compassion reaches out from the *zendo* wherever it will, and the needs of our time seem to be such that whenever environmental problems emerge and action has to be taken, the members of the Manila Zen Center are always asked to participate. It seems to be presumed that we sitters are developing an earth-consciousness. There is no doubt about the Source.

There is a story about an incident concerning India's Mother Teresa and a zealous young priest who wanted to work with her. At his first interview, he exclaimed how he loved the poor, that they were the chosen people and he wanted to help them, and so on. Finally Mother Teresa blurted out, 'You'd better get yourself well centred in God first, or you will die of frustration working with the poor.'

The present-day needs of the world require more than good-will. This may also be true of your own life. If you have felt at home while reading this book, and want to continue, search out the nearest Zen teacher. If there is no teacher available, then start sitting alone.

I occasionally interpreted for Yamada Roshi as he met with visitors from other lands. His contact with them might be for only an hour or two, but when asked for some instructions about sitting alone, he would always respond positively.

Yamada Roshi would teach the physical aspects of sitting, as outlined in the first chapter. He then taught breathing naturally, whilst counting inhalations and exhalations, cautioning that this might eventually become too busy a procedure. In such cases, watching the inhalation and counting the exhalation would be more satisfactory. There will be times when one can remain focused and one-pointed without counting. And his final exhortation was that breath-counting with perseverance, can lead one safely and surely to a true *kensho* experience.

If you are blessed by the presence of a true and able Zen teacher in your local community, then the first interview (*shoken*) will occasion the question 'Why do you want to do Zen?' The possible reasons are as all-embracing as the Way itself. Whatever had led you to persevere in reading to this point has probably found a home in what was said, and will generally be found sufficient by the teacher to welcome you as a disciple and a member of the *sangha*.

For the faithful practitioner, discipleship and membership grow and deepen, and one day, at a moment perhaps least expected, one comes to *know*:

> 'The Son can do nothing by himself; he can do only what he sees the Father doing; and whatever the Father does, the Son does too' (John 5:19).

And that fatherhood in activity is shared by all the family. Then and only then can we truly practise solicitous solidarity with all our other earth companions.

CHAPTER NINE

Who Am I?

W hat makes one choose Zen? Are there forerunners? How can you tell whether someone will be interested in Zen and be good at it? By that I mean, what kind of person will be at home in prayerful silence, and not in need of delicious things running around in the heart and mind or in and out of the senses, as part of one's daily meditation?

Whilst admitting that the therapeutic effects of an Oriental discipline will always be most welcome for all Occidentals, is there a special brand of Westerner who would be enriched by the new insights Zen brings, and find them complementary and helpful in one's own cultural heritage?

Is Zen meditation really prayer, and if it is, why do we need it? Have we not in Christianity a surfeit of different kinds of prayer that have nourished millions of people for two thousand years? What is prayer anyway? You keep saying Zen is different from Christian prayer, but if there's you and God, how is it different?

My Zen spirituality has been grounded in a specific experience which has led me to appreciate 'Unknowable' and 'Unnameable' as appropriate synonyms for the intimate God of my childhood. Why was I suddenly comfortable with such negations? The God who had been a lovable father, was now also the great Unknowable. One way to approach some of the above questions is to tell the story of how I came to 'know'.

And it is the Abhishiktananda's type of knowing as pointed out earlier in this volume ... it is the knowing of the Self, which experience, he says, is the highest possible attainment for a human being. Who am I really?

When asked to tell my Zen story, I always start by relating that I was born by the sea in Moncton, New Brunswick, in that part of Canada called The Maritimes. When I say 'by the sea', I am not referring to a location, I mean it as an experience, or to use Yamada Roshi's terminology, '*the true fact*'. Of course I always like the feel of moving through water, but the fact of the water is not a sensuous experience. There is a koan in the Blue Cliff Record which states that 16 Bodhisattvas came to experience *It* when they entered the bath. Water is another place of rendezvous.

I grew up in a musical family and have found music and the sea have much in common. In our small family orchestra, I came to delight in the inundation of rich harmonies in soaring and receding melodies. Musical capability is allowing all that potency to be adequately expressed. Maturity in music is getting the ego out of the way, and letting the inner flow 'one' it all together.

Parallel to this during my school years was the feel of the inner flow which sometimes happens to people in sport. Joseph Campbell has written of sport's spiritual identity. In fact one of the *zendo* members in Manila wrote an article for our annual diary there, *Zen and the Art of Running*. Is not all activity based in the spiritual? It took a long-time friend to 'see', just before I left Japan, that whilst I was playing the violin, IT extended right through into the instrument. IT had all become one.

Then in 1941, with university before me, my mind started to open. At a time when an older brother and sister were both at university, my parents felt financially constrained, and asked me to stay at home for a year. In reality, it turned out to be a time of adventure, a passage to adulthood, a journey into realms unknown, with attractive flags appearing on distant mountain peaks. However, I would not reach the foothills of the actual mountain for another 12 years or so.

This non-university year was spent in the company of books, or perhaps it would be more accurate to say, a time with great authors, whose learning never outshone their warmth of spirit. The books did not cover a wide range of subjects. They were predominantly religious by soul-free Catholics, enthusiastically hand-chosen by a cousin who had just left a Jesuit seminary. They were neither overtly theological nor specifically philosophical, and I thought them wonderful stories. I was full of delight in learning, seeing the world and living life with the eyes of sensitive, inquiring and appreciative people.

In those few months, I read most of the works of Hilaire Belloc, G.K. Chesterton, novels of R.H. Benson and some of Maurice Baring. I felt personally invited into their adventures and warmed to their subjects. I remember particularly Belloc's compassion when writing about Marie Antoinette's attempt at escape as the troops were closing in. Belloc took the trouble to research his subject so thoroughly that he went to the area where she was apprehended and, actually measuring the road and knowing the time, reported with regret that she probably could have made it had she taken the alternative path. And how intimate it felt to sit with GKC as he waited in a railway station, and reflected with humour and warmth on the trivial treasures he found in his pocket.

At a time when most people were appreciating the dark colours of Camus, I was devouring Peguy and Mauriac, and Maurois, and Bernanos, acquiring a taste of storytelling with a French touch. The clouds they described were never too dark for my spirit.

These new friends gave me a certain subtle appreciation of

the phenomenal world. And then occasionally there would be a sudden tug. Reading a short snippet of Pascal one day, the reference now forgotten, in a very direct way, I got beyond the words and was touched deeply within. I remember returning to that phrase again and again, and always recognizing something special in it. It was years before I knew the window to the mystic realm had been glimpsed. I understood that it was all right not to understand.

Suddenly, the path of music as a lifetime progession seemed doubtful. To my parents' consternation, I broached the idea of changing my major at college. When asked what I wanted to study, I recall being surprised to hear myself say 'philosophy'. It was a cause of great chagrin to me not to be able to answer their question of what I thought philosophy meant, except by saying that it dealt with ideas. Oh to have been a Sophie[14] who was told at 15 that a philosopher tries to grasp something that is eternal and immutable on the one hand, and the 'flow' on the other. Still, whilst not able to articulate the path, I was nevertheless treading it.

My parents suggested an aptitude test, and to *my* consternation, it suggested another inclination, this time towards journalism. Without this muddle ever resolved, I began a BA in English whilst majoring in violin at Mount Allison University in nearby Sackville. In two years I completed the requirements for a Licentiate in Music. There was something RIGHT about music after all, but I didn't know just what it was until I heard my Zen master say, 20 years later, that people who discipline themselves in artistic pursuits come to the Oriental religious experience more easily.

Going to Juilliard the following year acted as a catalyst: carrying my violin on the Broadway sidewalks between Columbia and the old Juilliard School, I could feel my life changing. Peak experience? Playing in a Piano Quartette with Arthur

Winograd doing the cello solo in a Brahms slow movement! And it wasn't just an emotional high. I grasped that day something of the eternally good, the eternally beautiful, and the eternally true. And daily I was touching another of *its* aspects, in the Juilliard corridors, bumping into other seeking students. Seeking what? No one could name it and the young people were both hesitating and running ahead in their search.

My home was with a cousin and her family in Teaneck, New Jersey. Her son Bill was the younger brother I had always wanted. Whilst introducing me to pizzas, he shared my attraction to philosophy. We did not know yet that it was in Hellenic times that philosophy moved into the area of 'salvation' and thus the boundaries between religion and philosophy were gradually eliminated. Back in the late forties, Bill and I were determined to fit the then-sure tenets of religion into our accompanying philosophy. We came to suspect that however our professional lives would emerge, we would only find fulfilment when we had found a philosophy that could tie all the aspects of our life together, and give us an answer to the many questions it held for us. So the search continued, though still solely an intellectual one.

Bill went on to Yale for his pre-med, and then chose Louvain for medicine, simply because he could continue the philosophy courses there. I envied his clarity of vision and purpose. I went on to Calgary, Alberta, having accepted a position on the staff of the Mount Royal College Conservatory of Music which provided scope for both performing and teaching.

Soon after arriving in the Canadian West, I met a young philosophy graduate called Ernie McCullough, who later was to go to the Medieval Institute in Toronto where he eventually got his Ph.D. With great enthusiasm, and starting with Plato and Aristotle, he led me through the minds of the philosophical giants.

To my surprise and sorrow, that part of my journey revealed there was no legitimacy in the search for a 'right' philosophy. I wanted truth in a package I could understand and accept intellectually. Instead, I was learning about the incomplete schools of thought of these great thinkers of the ages, and how TRUTH is an unfolding reality, and not a packaged deal.

One day, Ernie revealed that he was to try the priesthood. He had argued himself into thinking that it wasn't philosophy that counted most, but rather the kind of life one lived, one of service and dedication. At that time in history, the usual place for a young Catholic with such aspirations was the monastery or convent.

Robbed of the presence of this good friend, I went through the next few months in a state of wonder. Like so many young people of this era, I read Thomas Merton's autobiography, and he also seemed to be saying the same thing, using the Oriental metaphor, that learning is only the finger pointing to the moon. I do, however, recall being unmoved by his enthusiasm for the little classic of Thomas à Kempis, *The Imitation of Christ*. I was given John of the Cross to read, and one day, very quietly, I decided to try religious life. Just like that . . . no great vision, but I was later to say that I must have felt called. I chose a missionary order, because I loved to travel and meet adventure with peoples of other nations. Once again I was being led to something which held a great destiny for me. But I did not know it at the time, and said 'yes' for the above-mentioned reasons. Perhaps it was only Our Lady's Missionaries who could send me to the country which was to propel spiritual aspirations beyond the intellect. Certainly it was an 'in thing' at the time to go to the Orient.

By the second day in the convent, I had decided I would not stay. Community life went very much against the grain. I did not like what I was made to read and I certainly found no inspiration in the saints whose lives were read out to us daily. The treatises on prayer were dull and dead. For a great number of successive days, and for a number of reasons, I put off leaving until a more fortuitous time.

At some point in this period, a little book was put into my hands and the decision to leave became redundant. I hadn't changed any of my ideas of convent life but I had actually found what I was looking for. And it excited me. From that time onwards (a period which now spans 43 years) I was not to look back.

Here I was once again in a book, whose call I recognized immediately. The book is *One With Jesus*[15] by the Belgian Jesuit, Paul de Jaegher, in which he says there are two stages in the spiritual life. One is intimacy with Jesus and the other is what he calls identification, and what I later preferred to name as 'participation'. My suspicion of the idea of 'imitation' of Christ was confirmed.

De Jaegher describes identification as a mystical grace and tags it as Pauline spirituality. The practitioner gradually allows Christ to live and act freely within. In other words, we creatures actually share, even participate, in the existence of God.

In the Preface of this timely book, de Jaegher says,

If the soul is generous, this process of identification is often powerfully helped and fostered by a new mystical grace. To the feeling of his Divine Presence, God now adds the infused and passive feeling of his divine and transforming action. The soul feels that Christ lives and loves in her. She realizes in a experiential way that the infused love, which penetrates, absorbs and transports her whole being, is none other than the love with which Jesus himself loves his Father in her. She feels that her whole life is, as it were, fused in the life of Christ within her. She is one with him. And this identification, which at every step becomes more wonderful, leads to the perfect union of sanctity, that union which is called transforming, in which the soul can in very truth cry out with the Apostle: 'I live, now not I; but Christ liveth in me' (Galatians 2:20).[16]

(The Jerusalem Bible translation: I live now not with my own life, but with the life of Christ who lives in me.)

I believed with open mind and searching heart the core of de Jaegher's writing, especially the promise that God will make himself felt as an infused sense of the Divine Presence, which one 'tastes with delight'. One of the elements of this grace might truly be called dynamic, a dynamism which began with the immense love of the God-man and did not end with the grave. It is to be continued here on earth in people who will love with him until the ALL is completed ... only thus will the love-thirst of Christ for his Father be quenched. So we are indeed a continuation of the life of Jesus. We are truly other Christs, and created for union. To paraphrase an old Zen saying, it finally started to penetrate into my 72,000 pore holes, and gradually threw a special light on that biblical phrase which had always haunted me up until then that Christ liveth in me and is the source of the not-I. But it was some years before I could articulate it as saying the ego-self was to become no longer the agent of our actions.

Now I had only to find a teacher.

For three years in Novitiate, and five years of Juniorate, this not-I was my burning practice, an effort in lessening the strength of the ego. It was perhaps a beginning in mysticism, and also a language study for an encounter with Buddhism. However, my poor Novice Mistress's failure to find a teacher for me made it a lonely path.

During Juniorate it became increasingly clear that Our Lady's Missionaries' only mission for me was Japan. I longed to go there. During one low moment, having just read a delightful biography of Francis Xavier, I made a promise that if he got me to Japan, I would go up Mount Hiei overlooking Kyoto and be received there by a monk in lieu of the fact that Xavier had never been able to gain entrance to its temples.

Another lesson was an injunction from a young theologian, Michael Novak, earmarked at that time as liberal, who said to me upon leaving Canada, 'I hope you are going to Japan for one thing only, and that is to learn.' How right he was.

I arrived in Japan on 12 September, 1961. The following month I started Japanese language school in Kyoto, walking there within sightings of historic Mount Hiei. It was a daily reminder of the promise to Francis Xavier to visit the holy mountain in his stead. And on a cold March 25th, our day of Incarnation when we celebrate God's identity with the world, the long skirts of my habit were gathered up to battle the drifting snow on Hiei's peak, and eventually entered the grounds of the Tendai Buddhist gem of a temple, Shakado, to meet its famous guardian.

Horisawa Somon was a young Buddhist monk on *rosan*, a 12-year period of severe discipline, during which one must come to specific religious experiences. As a dedicated student at Kyoto University a few years previously, he had climbed his mountain literally on his 21st birthday, and subsequently had not returned to the world. In his deprivations and practice, he has been gifted to find the unfolding path of the spiritual journey. His is the light on the mountain top, to this day.

When we entered his presence that day in silence, he motioned us to seats around the *hibachi*, a deep Japanese brazier, and started to prepare tea. In serving, he used the movements known as 'butterfly', filling and setting the cups before myself and a friend. I knew Horisawa San was presenting something with this graceful serving, but *It* eluded me.

What seemed an hour later, he finally broke the silence by allowing my friend to make the introductions. When these were completed, he turned to me and asked very simply and earnestly, 'How do you pray?' I was nonplussed by his question, and asked what he meant. 'Well,' he replied, 'to start with, what position of the body do you recommend for prayer?' Somewhat relieved that he mentioned something so inconsequential, I brushed that consideration aside.

But Horisawa San would not be diverted, and stressed the body position as being very important for meditation. As the conversation unfolded, I learned about Zen for the first time. For all the strangeness in that Hieian temple 35 years ago, I had nevertheless come home, and Horisawa San and I continue to enjoy a very close friendship.

After language school, I studied music terms in Japanese at the Jesuit Elizabeth School of Music in Hiroshima. Its founder and Director smiled knowingly as he said, 'And besides, I shall give you a spiritual director who is a mystic in both the Western and Eastern traditions, Fr Hugo Enomiya-Lassalle.' This distinguished man had been rector of the parish church which was almost directly under the epicentre of the atomic bomb when it fell over Hiroshima in August 1945. He had his story partially told by John Hersey in the book *Hiroshima*, which appeared in the *New Yorker* magazine, and reappeared in countless books and articles. It seems that everyone got to know Fr Lassalle, as he is lovingly called.

A non-Japanese does not easily become a citizen of that country, but Fr Lassalle, having mercifully recovered from the injuries sustained during the bomb blast, rebuilt his church so magnificently with funds gathered the world over, that the Japanese government honoured him with citizenship. The name he chose used the ideograms for love and temple.

When I met him, knowing none of this, one of the first

questions I asked was if he knew anything about Zen. To my embarrassment, I learned that he had been sitting with Zen monks and under the famous Harada Roshi for many years. I placed myself immediately at his feet, along with thousands of other disciples around the world, and most lovingly dedicate this book to his memory, in gratitude for the 'love of the temple' to which he was able to lead many of us. I had finally found my teacher.

My missionary apostolate for the Japanese was to be a Culture Centre just outside the city of Osaka, in an industrial town called Suita. We taught mainly Western classical music, but many of the Japanese arts were also taught in this small compound. Like most zealous missioners, I dived into them with great gusto, but soon found out that gusto is not a requisite in Japanese culture.

There are many books by Occidentals who practised Japanese arts in that country, but none more famous or graphic than Eugene Herrigel's *Zen and the Art of Archery*. The author reasoned that since shooting had been his sport in Germany, during his teaching assignment in Japan, it would perhaps be most auspicious to study *kyudo* (archery). His whole book is the agony of passing from the 'aiming' of gun practice to the 'not-aiming' secret of archery.

The first art I tried was the *okoto* or Japanese harp which sits on the floor. It has over a dozen strings, and one can play the whole melody of *Sakura* (Cherry Blossoms) without depressing a string! I progressed quickly, and was soon asked to play in a large *kaikan*, a kind of concert hall, in Osaka with about a hundred other harpists. Shortly after this recital, I was told the next step was to sing, not as I have always sung, but using a kind of falsetto, which reminded me of Swiss yodelling. I immediately recognized this was not for me, so next changed my study to *sado*, the Japanese tea ceremony. That lasted only two or three months, for when told I must walk seven steps to cover the distance of three yards, I looked at my long legs and large feet and said I didn't think they could manage that gracefully. Then I tried *shodo*, writing Japanese ideographs, where one does nothing at first but learn to hold the brush so that the *It* power flows evenly from body into arm and hand, to the brush and ink and onto the paper. When one can doodle satisfactorily, we can proceed to number one. Three years of doodling without even getting to one, would that make me a mystic?

The only perseverance came with *kado*, flower arranging or ikebana, as it is best known, but even after 10 years, the teacher was still choosing, cutting, and arranging the flowers first. Of course inwardly I rebelled.

What did all this lack of initiative do for me? Was it a necessary step to deepening in Zen? Yes it was. I was aware of being taught to let the power within act of itself without hindrance of ego. I was not being taught not to use the ego. I was being taught to allow the not-I to act. At long last, the 'I live now not I' was coming into daily life.

During this time, I was regularly going to sit with the Zen nuns at Enkoji in north Kyoto, which Fr Lassalle had arranged. Nowadays there is nothing novel about a Westerner going to a Buddhist temple to learn Zen. But for me in the early sixties, there was quite an adjustment to be made. Enkoji was a combination of what we would call the novitiate and mother house. All *sesshin* were given there, and I found the severity of the horarium almost beyond human endurance. Up at 3 a.m. and chanting by 3.05, the schedule went on until midnight.

I was not at home in the *Rinzai* harshness but now I am grateful for its strength, and the opportunity for lots of sitting in meditation with others. There were no great insights, no special understandings, and certainly no sweetness. There *was* lots of cold. However, somehow I knew something long desired was happening and the thought of quitting never entered my mind. But years later when I was happily ensconced under Yamada Koun Roshi, I was able to nod assent to his frequent assertion that there is no satori experience without sore knees.

As related earlier in this text, one day in the early seventies, I was sitting with Fr Lassalle at his beautiful *zendo* Shinmeikutsu west of Tokyo. I experienced aural *makyo*, and he suggested that I go to a different teacher who could help me through the experience. His recommendation was to a man becoming well known in the Japanese Zen scene of the day, Yamada Koun Roshi. I had an interview with him the following day, and was accepted as a disciple.

In December of that year, I went to Kamakura, for the *Rohatsu Sesshin*, an eight-day retreat prior to the anniversary of the Buddha's enlightenment. We had daily *dokusan* and when the Roshi would thrust out a *koan*, my responses were very commonplace. But on December 5, I found myself responding to one of the Roshi's thrusts differently. He immediately proceeded to change his focus, but he couldn't budge me after the first shift.

The Roshi tried several angles to again get me moving, as this period is often called in Zen. At the next *dokusan*, he completely surprised me by asking, 'Where is God?' I pointed to my heart. He thrust out his hand and said, 'Isn't God also in the little finger?' and immediately he rang his handbell to conclude the interview.

Back in my sitting place in the *zendo*, I looked at my neglected finger-tips. For all my yearning to appreciate God dwelling 'there', the stronger pull was right over the heart, and I was uneasy. I asked to speak with Fr Lassalle who was also participating in the *sesshin*. His advice was to have utter confidence in the Roshi and the method he was using.

I resumed my practice and was soon on track again. In the

early evening of 6 December, as the stars began to come out, that heart-spot burst open, and its beautiful contents exploded right through the whole of me, until there was no-Elaine left. This grasping of 'not-I' was an experience of intense happiness, and for several weeks my short gatha (prayerful verse) was daily on my lips. 'This joy, this perfect joy, was now mine' (John 3:29). The Jerusalem Bible translation reads, 'This same joy I feel, and now it is complete.'

I rushed down to the *dokusan* (interview) line-up, and shortly was admitted into the Roshi's presence. His smile broadened until it matched my own, and he started the age-old examination for one who has had an authentic experience. He confirmed mine immediately. Finally the gate had opened, and to my great delight, I found there had never been one there at all. There is always free access to the source of love. Kneeling in front of this Buddhist master with bursting heart, I KNEW I had just touched IT. How appropriate that the dictionary meaning of satori is 'to know'.

A religious experience where you see nothing, hear nothing, and touch nothing, is difficult to convey. But I realized then the reason for articulating it with negatives. It is, however, a negative that is full of potential! Words may define the event, they give no indication of its content or moment of great joy.

The opening insight of *kensho* is usually just a peep-hole. Then comes a post-*kensho koan* study which deepens and enlarges the sightings. I soon went to live in Kamakura, so that I could be in the presence of the Roshi every day. I earned enough to cover living expenses by teaching English, as most North Americans did in Japan at that time. There were 20 or 25 'foreigners' who had given up everything to live in Kamakura and sit in meditation under a great teacher. Half of these were religious nuns and priests, and the joy of camaraderie was high.

There was Ruben Habito, a Filipino of exceptional intellectual ability, who became the first Catholic to have his experience confirmed and encouraged it to flower into compassionate service of the poor. Willigis Jager in true Benedictine hospitality would hold open house daily for sitting and lauds and mass and breakfast. And we all gathered together, Joan Rieck and Sister Kathleen Reiley, and Paul Shepherd, and Ursula Okle and Rainer Holdt and Niklaus Brantschen and Ama Samy and others. We filled the *zendo* (26 mats) nightly, and ended by sharing tea with the Roshi and his gracious wife, usually listening to Beethoven or some new record this music-loving Zen teacher had just purchased.

Thanks to the Roshi and my Jesuit pianist friend Larry McGarrell, I not only returned to modest solo violin work, but through much sharing and mutuality, saw how it is part of the woof and weave of my spiritual journey. Life and living *is* the flow . . . nothing different from what it had always been, but all the difference in the world to experience. This was indeed the fullness of the immutability and the eternal, along with the flow that philosophy had once promised. I was always grateful for the gift of the great Roshi and gradually the richness of relationships with other Zen sitters struck me in full force.

Eventually the highs and lows receded and life became ordinary again, but I knew beyond the shadow of a doubt that Jesus and the great spiritual teachers through the ages had not deceived me.

To return to those questions asked at the beginning of this chapter. What made me choose Zen? I don't feel I chose it, but rather it chose me. Were there steps or signposts along the way? Well, all the events described in this chapter are, I think, relevant and leading to that moment of KNOWING.

Finally a word or two about prayer. Training in the Japanese language has its own difficulty in this field. Its word for 'prayer' is *inoru*, but any Zen master will assert that Zen meditation is not *inoru*. I seem to have imbibed this distinction myself. I tend to use prayer for any relationship with God, using the faculties of the psyche, the intellect, the memory, emotions, imagination, etc. To silence all these into a focus of absorption of the breath, coupled with a silent body, is the beginning of meditation. I feel that God's gift to the Orient is in the potency of silence, in which we might experience his power, and allow him to live again on earth. It seems to me now, this is what de Jaegher's book is all about. This very book is my personal articulation of just that. And no description is more cogent than the Roshi's own articulation that prayer is light sitting in light.

Spirituality Today

In 1976, I was sent to be a missioner to the Philippines, to Leyte, an island of very poor farmers and fisherfolk. Their physical situation was appalling, the children hungry, the tenant farmers oppressed, the whole country in a state of siege by the rapacious Marcos family. To help in the Filipinos' bid for a sustainable food programme, I studied biodynamic farming.

This new method of farming was taught as the latest step in the long development of agriculture, and the teacher, Nicanor Perlas, frequently used the Greek word, *aletheia*. He said it represented 'truth from the divine oracle' in the sense of it being revealed only gradually.

Within the field of agriculture, we learned the different steps in the unveiling of the most appropriate way to cultivate the soil, and how these procedures had changed throughout history. Two decades ago chemical farming was the miracle of the day, until it was found to be not sustainable. Then we turned to organic farming, which is in harmony with the earth and its environments. Today, biodynamic farming is possibly the 'last word' in the unfolding in this field, and interestingly, in accord with the ancient agricultural practices of the tribal people in the mountainous areas of the northern Philippines. They have known for centuries of the life-force at work in nature, a kind of spirituality of the soil. I came to learn that, like the sea, earth too is a rendezvous.

In 1994, I heard Fritjof Capra speak at St James' in Piccadilly, about the *aletheia* in physics. His field is subatomic particles, and when giving the historic evolutions that had taken place in science, he said when it moved out of the mechanistic model, 'it wasn't that it was wrong', there was just a new insight, new knowledge. The curtain had been pulled back a bit, and more of truth had been revealed, so that physics moved on to the different level of recognizing some particles as being only energy and not matter, as was formerly thought. Are we here touching the spirituality of matter?

For Martin Heidegger, *aletheia* is uncovering what is real. The emergence of the real is the life-force in all of creation, and it seems to me, that is what spirituality is. I like to call it our 'lifing'.

It's just like having a vast statue swathed in cloth, and gradually the cloth is being pulled away, and the figure revealed, not all at once, but bit by bit. And we don't damn the part that was revealed yesterday which was, of course, incomplete, for so is our bit 'today'. At some points in history, there seems to be an extra emerging spurt, which presents a dramatic change from that which preceded, and is called a new world-view or paradigm. We are frequently told that our today is witnessing such a dramatic change. Some see us witnessing the demise of many of our structures, in government and politics and morals and family life, etc. And perhaps deeper than all of these, religion as we have known it for the last thousand years seems to be coming to an end, or at least to a new beginning.

Anyone interested in spirituality today, and the vast paradigm changes we are undergoing at the moment, HAS to be free to be part of the flow. Often it is a blind leap, such as my decision to do Buddhist meditation. I really did not know what I was getting into.

At Capra's lecture, he asked for questions on a point made,

and one woman said hesitatingly, 'I'm very confused and don't know just how to articulate what is bothering me...' Dr Capra immediately interrupted, 'My dear lady, we are all in the process of change and in that sense confused, because we have no clear sightings yet. Just try to give us a feeling of what you want to say, and many of us will be right there with you, believe me!'

Anyone who is unwilling to identify with that statement will perhaps be inimical to what follows about Zen in the West. Because we too are in beginnings, we too are sometimes confused, and there are weeks when every step seems to be uncharted.

Despite having been designated as a Zen teacher, I have not become a Buddhist. Neither am I a theologian, so I feel reticent to articulate my experience in theological terms. However I am a Christian, and understand myself to have a Christian spirituality, which has been augmented by my practice of Zen. Zen has been represented innumerable times so far in this text as being in the field of religious experience. I find it appropriate now to sometimes use negative designations for God, which has to do with semantics and not value.

The introduction to this book states that the historian Arnold Toynbee once said that the meeting of Buddhism and Christianity would be one of the most important events in the twentieth century. An interesting aside is that I have not met anyone who knows the source of that particular aphorism, although it can be easily assumed from his writings. We are now edging towards the end of the particular time-frame of the twentieth century, and can discern that Buddhism and Christianity have met, with several consequences.

There is the fact that within the last half-century, many Christians and Catholics (especially after Vatican II), went to the trouble of going to Japan, learning the language, searching out an able and true teacher, spending years participating in the practice of the Buddhist meditation called Zen, and being led to its experience. I have personally been doing this for almost 35 years. What follows is an account of my own experiences, supported by other Western companions. I place it all in the field of spirituality.

When I went to Japan in 1961, I became involved in inter-religious dialogue. At first there was the language problem, but now, 35 years later, I can't recall even having a moment's thought that dialogue would of necessity be with any Japanese, other than Christians. There was no exchange at that time between Christians and Buddhists beyond the social or academic levels. That was the point of *aletheia* before Vatican II. They went their way, and we went ours.

I met Buddhist nuns and liked them, and wanted to interact with them at some level, later deciding on meditation. But the dialogue was with other Christians, and very soon we found ourselves at an impasse, for there were no issues to debate. Amongst ourselves, we had no fight with dogma or sacrament. It wasn't long before we decided that our interaction would be in the field of social action, which as Christians in the sixties and seventies, was the popular and contemporary choice.

Gradually, good news from the Vatican Council began to seep out, and we were invited to make a leap. No longer was it the spirit of 'them and us'. In order to understand our new freedom, one must picture us in the late sixties, amidst the euphoria of Vatican II. It ended in 1965, but it took two or three or four more years to disseminate its tenets, and put them into practice. I was one of several missionaries in Japan, basking in the statement, which had already become part of our lived experience through close association with Buddhists. There was indeed 'a ray of the Truth which enlightens all men' in Buddhism. I felt I had found one.

Another important discovery of the time was to find that not everyone was excited by the news. Even though my own community, Our Lady's Missionaries, is a Foreign Missionary Society, most of our sisters did not feel personally touched by the new articulation of the Church's attitude towards other religions. That we should dialogue with and learn from Buddhists, seemed a real shift to me. It seemed however to speak eloquently to some people, and to others not at all. I now think that at this point in time, perhaps Zen will appeal to people of a certain temperament. And as far as mission is concerned, many of the Japanese Christians in the parish I served were hostile to the time I spent in Buddhist Temples. Some were indifferent. A very few were gladdened.

I am finding the same in England today. I now give meditation workshops in prisons for the Prison Phoenix Trust. Many chaplains and prison officers cannot understand the spiritual value of the disciplines of yoga and meditation. Others are indifferent and a few are enthusiastic.

There is some antipathy by both Buddhists and Christians. The former seem either to resent intrusion of territory or simply do not understand how a non-Buddhist can sit in Zen meditation whilst not adopting the tenets of its religion. I find it very interesting that it is the Buddhist leaders of the Sanbo Kyodan who are meeting this problem with the clear articulation that Zen transcends religion, nationality, culture and gender. How can there be conflict in a silent mind?

Christians often cannot understand how a Christian can do a Buddhist meditation and still remain a Christian. This is understandable to a degree, because Christian meditation usually has an object which is Christ. The fact that Zen is a meditation without an object seems perhaps too facile a response. But there it is. It comes down to silencing the ego, where we do not do, but rather we *allow*.

So what is this spirituality for Christians? To quote a friend and Jesuit priest, 'For Christians, spirituality is nothing other than a life in attunement to the Spirit, the breath of God, where we let our total being be taken up in its dynamic presence. Paying attention to our breathing in meditation, is seen not simply as a physical exercise that keeps us concentrated on one point, but as the very abandonment of our total being to the breath of God here and now.'

There is another related point that begs attention, the problem of the sect of Buddhism called Zen Buddhism. I have many Christian and Buddhist friends who say that Zen Buddhism is not a religion, and that a Christian can remain one whilst becoming a Zen Buddhist. This appears to be an idealistic reading of the facts. Historically, Zen started in China, a radical effort to return to the purity of Shakyamuni's original intent. Yamada Roshi always used to say that the Buddha never intended to start a religion. I am aware that the following is probably over-simplifying, but the Buddha taught that one had only to come to experience to realize the way things ARE. Consequent to this, one learns HOW ONE SHOULD LIVE LIFE in the light of that experience.

Be that as it may, and whatever the founders of Zen Buddhism meant it to be, the fact is that it is now a religion, with 'things that can be written down' as Yasutani Roshi used to say. Not only can one become a Zen Buddhist without having had the experience, but almost all the Zen Buddhists in Japan never meditate, nor endeavour to come to satori.

During that spectacular event in London in 1994, when the Dalai Lama participated in a Christian Meditation retreat, he very carefully and forcefully stated that Catholicism is a religion and Buddhism is a different religion, and we should not try to mix them. To use his graphic phrase for those who call themselves Buddhist-Christians, they are trying to put a yak's head on a sheep's body.

So I, a Catholic, sat in Zen meditation under two Zen

Buddhist masters, who endeavoured to help people come to the specific experience which shows us how things are, and by its light, live in that reality. The first was Fukagai Gichu, the Roshi at the *Rinzai* nuns' temple, Enkoji, in northern Kyoto. Zen describes itself as:

A special transmission outside the scriptures;
No dependence upon words and letters;
Directly pointing to the mind;
Seeing into one's nature and the realization of Buddhahood.

Fukagai Roshi was in true *Rinzai* transmission. However, she was not a talented teacher, and during her 23 years at Enkoji, was never able to bring any of her nuns to the opening experience of *kensho*, and the *koan* study which follows. Thus with her death in 1985, the temple was appropriated by the *Rinzai* monks and set up as an architectural showpiece. In the delicious quirks one often encounters in life, the *kotsu* (the slightly curved teaching stick a *roshi* carries for ceremonies) of this last woman *Rinzai* roshi was given by her nuns, not to one of their own number, but to her one former disciple now teaching who was neither Japanese nor Buddhist, but a Canadian Catholic nun.

Yamada Koun Roshi, a layman educated at the Dai-ichi High School in Tokyo and later at its prestigious Tokyo University, did not start Zen until his late thirties, when he was caught in Manchuria by the Second World War. Once he had sighted the mountain, he never let the beckoning flow of the flag out of his view. There are few lay people in the annals of great Zen personages, nevertheless he was always proud to be a layman, a businessman, a father and grandfather. With diligent practice, he eventually came to an extremely deep experience of satori, and was chosen to lead the newly formed sect of Zen Buddhism, the Sanbo Kyodan. Its actual founder was Harada

Roshi, mentioned earlier as the teacher of Fr Lassalle. It incorporated the best of *Rinzai* and *Soto* Zen, both of which he perceived were dying away.

Yamada Roshi had great admiration for Western culture and the religion from which it sprang, namely Christianity. He was very keen that his Christian disciples remain practising Christians, and gradually bring true Zen into its spiritual treasure-house.

The subject of this book does not have to do with Buddhism as a religion, but with Zen, which I see as the mysticism of Buddhism, aware all the while of mysticism's possible divisions. The adjunct of that view posits ethics, for it is useless to practise Zen and not put it to work in one's life. Its ethics evolve from the 'appropriate' and not the realm of right or wrong. Sitting under a Zen Buddhist master did not flinch my moral code an inch, except perhaps to become more sensitive.

The practice of Zen has become very popular in the second half of this twentieth century. There are centres for meditation all over the world. Some people have been unrealistic in their need for change and have flocked to any centre calling itself a *zendo*. This has prompted well-meaning people with little knowledge of Zen to lead groups. In time, this leadership presents real power, a great seduction in anyone's life, but particularly towards the vulnerable. As has often been said, there is no arrogance like spiritual arrogance. Hence spiritual direction is fertile ground for the many abuses of that power, particularly sexual misconduct in the teacher-disciple relationship.

Despite some bogus teaching, there are several teachers, whilst not part of a legitimate transmission, who give *sesshin* (Zen retreats), a healthy programme of silent sitting, nutritious food, and yoga *asanas*. Undoubtedly this leads to many benefits, but does one ever come to really know the answer to 'who am I?'

Since coming to England, I have become more aware of the presence of Theravada groups. The monasteries are flourishing and multiplying, although the long-term presence is still hanging in the balance. There are also several Buddhist societies which have flourished here for a hundred years. There has been a presence of *Rinzai* Zen for some years in the middle of London, ideally placed to offer regular sitting░░░░░░░░░░ *dokusan*. There is a *Soto* group up in the northeast of ░░░ try, which seems to be in the present *Soto* tradition found t░░░ in Japan. But this group, as many others, have formed themselves around the monastic system and are inclined to give spiritual direction to their special disciples and student monks and nuns only.

There is also the growing presence of the Tibetan monks and nuns here and all over the world. Part of this is undoubtedly due to the popularity of the Dalai Lama. But those who have moved close to him assure us that he has stern words for para-Buddhists, and is very strict that Buddhism not be misrepresented. In other words, he is aware of the self-made teachers who are dropping ashes in the outstretched hand of Buddhist statues. The political problems of Tibetans impels them towards a massive financial drive to educate their young men, a tradition very strong in their culture. This has undoubtedly made them somewhat more evangelical than they would normally be. All these groups, with the exception of *Rinzai*, encourage conversion, and many Westerners have become Buddhists.

Perhaps the closest Zen Buddhists to me are the Japanese and ancient Chinese masters, and there I have met many spiritual giants. There is considerable despair over present-day Japanese Zen Buddhism. But much the same is heard of almost all world religions. The groanings and creakings of the barque of St Peter too are often heard, as it laboriously tries to contain its members. Here in England the national church has to account for itself daily, as its physical buildings crumble. There is hardly a religion or spirituality in today's world untouched by the pain involved in the period of change we are undergoing. It is not the prerogative of any one sect. Let us not cast stones, nor see the mote in another's eye. I recall the candour of an American ▓▓▓▓▓▓▓▓▓▓▓ Church and became a Tibetan nun 23 years ▓▓▓▓ ʌnat she has found in Buddhism all the structures ▓▓pression and sexual abuse that caused her to leave the Church, many years before. But she is older and wiser now and does not quit. Much of this is due to her personal regard for His Holiness the Dalai Lama, but also, I suspect she has persevered in her own spirituality and found strength and hope and peace.

As do I. In these days of sensationalism and woundedness, we can perhaps understand why hope is one of the cardinal virtues. It is found in the most unexpected places. Living in the Philippines during some of its most difficult years, we all seemed freed by the spirit within. The years leading to their splendid revolution, were a lesson in the hope and courage that pain and poverty can spawn. Ruben Habito describes it in a Zen way as reaching the zero point. The Filipinos had done all they could. Now it was in another's hands. They moved beyond their ego.

I find today that there is much hope in prison work. Many of the inmates have reached their zero point, and turn their world upside down, by seeking their inner freedom there. Whatever your idea of a prison incarceration, it was a lifer who wrote to us, **'Who could ever imagine a man's freedom being found in prison!'** Wisdom can seep in despite or because of anxiety and pain.

As I write, there is a man of 25 dying in a nearby prison by his own choice. He was a hopeless son, a cruel husband and an abusive father, a murderer and rapist. Following his conviction, he asked for and received help, eventually wanting to make amends for all the crimes he had committed. He is fasting unto death. He took out a legal injunction against the prison hospital staff and they are not allowed to touch him, unless he asks for something. He is full of peace!

Yeah! You were right when you said that when you feel you are going to crack up is just the time that sometimes things begin to take a new and better turn. They have for me...y meditation book...I learn something every day.

I teach meditation in a therapeutic prison once a week. I am frequently asked how I regard therapy and have come to believe in its process as long as it is holistic. It must have a spiritual element for the 36 men on the Wing. One of my meditators is the cook, and we talk about certain foods being peace-giving. When he was two, his mother committed suicide, and four, when his alcoholic father turned him out on the streets, and finally at fourteen, he was convicted of armed robbery. Once in prison, he rebelled continuously, accumulating a terrible prison record, attacking officers and once even the governor himself. He was moved 15 times in four years, went on dirty protest, and then his cell-mate hanged himself. Soon afterwards he wrote saying he wanted to get his head together, so our correspondence took a new direction, and eventually he ended up in Grendon, the country's principal therapeutic prison, where he is finally getting the help he desires and needs.

There is plenty of pressure in prison but most of it is made by myself which I never realized before. Now I really look forward to my period of meditation.

Speaking of holistic approaches, I feel this must happen right across the board. I happen to be working with offenders. But I am in touch with others who work with the victims, and for a holistic healing, both offender and victim (or victim's family) must be bonded. And then there is the judiciary: a judge has the law to defend, but judgement depends not only on the nature of the crime but also on its cause. It came as no surprise therefore to have been asked by one of the judges if I would consider meditation seminars for them. Another prisoner wrote:

I can only say that what I saw as a hopeless situation, has now become a blessing to my spiritual growth. I have begun to enjoy this life...it's a perfect setting for practising meditation and yoga.

That is why meditation is such an appropriate aid for prisoners. It cuts down inner blocks in a gradual way, and simultaneously seems to burst into inner spark and frees life! Not only does it act therapeutically, but it also is the Way of the Sacred. Of all the mail I have received in the last year, nothing moved me more than one young 22 year old who wrote:

As long as I can remember, I have had this hurt inside. I can't get away from it, and sometimes I cut or burn myself so that the pain will be in a different place and on the outside. Then I saw the Prison Phoenix Trust Newsletter last month, and something spoke to me about meditation and although I didn't really know what it is, I wrote for your book. I just want you to know that after only 4 days of meditating a half hour in the morning and at night, for the first time in my life, I see a tiny spark of something within myself that I can like.

That tiny hidden spark! It is that flag on the distant mountain for us all, and the source of all our yearning. Where do I find IT now that I have come to England? Not only in prisons, but of course in many hidden corners of an English garden, in churches and chapels and willows overhanging streams, in the brown furrows of spring and the golden-ness of harvest, in the open space of the Highlands, and in gentle English writings. The other day, a friend from Essex sent me a copy of Herbert's Prayer where IT is:

> the Churches' banquet
> angels' age
> heart in pilgrimage
> sinners' tower
> reversed thunder
> Christ's side-piercing spear

The mystic sightings are often best expressed through nature, and at the end of my formal study with Yamada Koun Roshi, he asked about a phrase which is found in the last book of training, 'The Ittai Sanbo, the Three Treasures in One Body, what is it after all?' and I quoted the famous lines of Dogen which over the years are gradually becoming my own:

> I came to realize clearly
> that Mind is no other
> than mountains, and rivers,
> and the great wide earth,
> the sun and the moon and the stars.

And with great delight, I indulged in a favourite joy, quoting a Christian parallel from John of the Cross:

> My beloved is the mountains,
> And lonely wooded valleys,
> Strange islands,
> And resounding rivers,
> The whistling of love stirring breezes.

An Interview

This interview between Sister Elaine MacInnes and a group of about 100 young people was conducted at the Tibetan Amitabha Buddhist Centre in Singapore, March 1992. The Buddhist nun in charge introduced Sister Elaine and then asked her to tell the group the facts of her life which would be of interest and help during the evening's dialogue.

Sr EM: There are a few facts of the ambience in which I have developed spiritually, that strike me as important, if I am to tell my story. The rest will be sharing in a question-and-answer period. But first I'd like to ask the first two questions right now: How many of you here come from a Christian background? [More than two-thirds of the audience raise their hands.] How many come from a Buddhist background? [The same majority laughingly responded. Regarding this, Sister Elaine later remarked: 'So it turned out we had a lot in common!']

The first point I always mention is that I was born by the sea, which I have learned is more than a location. Also, I had no argument with religion; at that time and place the Catholic Church was still warm and secure, and harboured many able custodians who kept it a natural habitat for my growing, inquisitive and enthusiastic spirit. I chose music as my profession, and this kept the spirit finely tuned. I went abroad, and lived amongst people of a very different and rich culture at a time when the Vatican Council helped to put it in focus for me.

Q: Would you tell us where you first heard about Zen?

Sr EM: I first heard about it at the beautiful Shakado Temple on the top of Mount Hiei overlooking the city of Kyoto. I learned it from the Buddhist nuns with whom I sat for a few years.

Q: What is Zen?

Sr EM: Ah, that's the toughest question of all. Because we are all seekers here this evening, I would probably answer that Zen is experiencing fully and at all times. It is the Way, the Tao, the Michi of the Orient. On the cushion, Zen is to sit in a prescribed position, concentrating in one-pointed breath awareness. Away from the cushion, Zen is what the Buddhists call 'awareness of being' which is a kind of alertness to the present moment. If I could, I would use that word 'being' as electrically charged, for that might illustrate what spirit and spirituality is.

Q: What is *kensho*?

Sr EM: Literally, *kensho* is to see our nature. In the line of what I have just said, *kensho* is to experience that 'electric charge'. There are many depths to *kensho*, and I have found after many years of teaching, that we usually have 'custom-made' *kensho*, if you know what I mean.

Q: Can you tell us how you check for *kensho*?

Sr EM: Sorry! The teaching process in Zen is esoteric.

Q: As a Christian, did you articulate your experience differently from Buddhists?

Sr EM: No and yes! Because he had disciples from all over the world and many different religions, Yamada Roshi frequently used any number of tags for the realities we were dealing with. And following a *kensho* experience, we tended to use the same words. But the Roshi, a great admirer of Catholicism, was very keen that Zen come into the Church, and he encouraged us Catholics to work together for an articulation that would speak to us all. We are still in process and gradually a vocabulary is evolving, and something beautiful is taking shape. I presume though that it will take decades for Zen to be fully integrated within the institutional Church.

Q: Do you find any problems practising Zen as a Christian?

Sr EM: Yamada Roshi always insisted that Zen is not a religion. And as to Buddhism, I am quite ignorant. If I may answer your question, no, I have not found any problems in practising true Zen as a practising Christian.

Q: Then would you say that your Church allows this?

Sr EM: The Asian bishops go further than allowing, they encourage it.

Q: Are you sure you're a Catholic nun? [*Great laughter.*]

Sr EM: I've been under that impression for forty years.

Participant: I'm a member of the *zendo* here that Sister Elaine has been leading for eleven years, and although

I can't prove she is a Catholic nun, I can say that she always speaks like this.

Q: I understand the Filipino Church is socially oriented. How do you sponsor this with Japanese Zen which is not so inclined?

Sr EM: The Zen Way always combines wisdom and compassion. In this regard, the lives of the first Zen monks in Japan were living testimony to compassion as they established schools and hospitals and built roads, etc. And in contemporary times, my own teacher Yamada Koun Roshi worked in a hospital by day which necessitated three hours commuting to and from Tokyo, and then returned home to give us *dokusan* each evening. Also, I think cultures vary a great deal. The social activity of the Filipinos was catapulted into action partly by the political situation.

Q: What are the indications that a breakthrough is close?

Sr EM: Well, one is *makyo*, those manifestations in the subconscious which surface sometimes. There is often an unaccountable flow of tears. And I often can tell from a person's physical sitting that they are advancing into deeper areas of consciousness.

Q: Do lights come from the body?

Sr EM: No, not in Zen.

Q: What about the different perception you mentioned before? How do you perceive differently?

Sr EM: Perhaps the best articulation is that we get glimpses, very fleetingly and incomplete, but still glimpses, of the Truth that all phenomena are empty, and the other and I are not separate. But all this happens after 'you' have disappeared. I recall one of our monitors at Kamakura saying that wonderful things can happen when we disappear.

Q: As a Christian, you believe that God is a person, don't you?

Sr EM: Yes, I believe God is person, but since that word 'believe' is somewhat embattled today, I would also like to say that I feel I have experienced God as person.

Q: But I understand the mystical experience of *kensho* is not of God as person. Did you find that to be so in your *kensho*?

Sr EM: I would articulate *kensho* as an experience of the power of God, and yes, that is non-personal.

Q: Well isn't that a problem for you?

Sr EM: Not really. The part of the paradigm change we have already experienced has brought us out of 'either-or' into the 'both-and' category. The Church has always taught that God is both transcendent and immanent, but somehow the former seemed to dominate in our religion. Now I feel more spiritually balanced.

Q: So you can be both Christian and Buddhist?

Sr EM: Now you're back into religions!

Q: Well, where are you?

Sr EM: I'm in the field of what we call spirituality. My spirituality is a combination of Western Christianity, which teaches me to relate to God who is transcendent, and Oriental spirituality, which teaches me how to commune with the immanent God.

Q: But doesn't the oppressive masculinity of the Christian God get to you?

Sr EM: As you probably know, the matrix of Christianity is Judaism, which was often strongly masculine. And being a woman in the world and of this time and place, I am more comfortable with the non-sexist terminology. God is not masculine, not feminine, and both, and I'm always trying to speak in those terms. But it is difficult to refer to God as masculine for 40 years and then make such a shift in reference. You might be interested to know that our community recites the ancient Hebraic psalms using inclusive terminology. And the feminine issue is one of our concerns.

Q: Could you speak more of the complementarity of God's transcendence and immanence in prayer?

Sr EM: Because of our creaturehood, we relate to God as children and 'Father' a most beneficent provider (as we are finding out in our ecological studies). We are therefore relational, so in a sense God has to be 'other'... So, I can think about God, I can feel about God, I can remember, and I can love God, as we used to say, in thought, word and deed.

When I became a sister, I found I sometimes easily tired of words and feeling in prayer, and sought for a teacher in what we call contemplative prayer, not using words or feeling. It was not until I came to the Orient that I found one, and to my delight and surprise, I realized that the Oriental Way is all about the Immanent God, with whom all creation is ONE and therefore not in a position of relationship, but of communion. For me it is no longer 'either-or' but 'both-and'. I am very grateful for this.

Q: Did any of the Christian mystics have a *kensho*, do you think?

Sr EM: The articulation of some of our mystics leads me to think they had that same experience – John of the Cross, Meister Eckhart and Tauler, for example. I often tell Christians that a Buddhist taught me what John of the Cross means by his frequent use of *nada*, the Spanish word for 'nothing'.

Q: Do you think Buddhists are hunting for the person of God?

Sr EM: Shibayama Roshi, in his book *A Flower Doesn't Talk*, says that when the Japanese use the term *Hotoke*, their reference is to a Buddha very similar to the God of the Christians. But as I said before, I'm not a Buddhist scholar, and I don't know much more than that. I have read one or two articles by Buddhists who seek a unity with Christianity, but I do not understand all the subtleties of their thought.

Q: To whom do you address your proselytizing?

Sr EM: I do not proselytize, and traditionally, there is no advertising in Zen. If people ask, I answer from my experience. Nor do I go out and recruit disciples. I teach Zen to those who want to learn to sit and come to experience. Our group of teachers from the Kamakura Sanbo Kyodan do not sanitize Zen, but rather teach it as we received it. This is most important for me, because I seem to be about the only member of the group working with people of another culture than my own, so it is very important for me to stick to the essentials and not slip into associations, otherwise I might take my disciples on a trip through Canada.

Q: Why do you keep referring to the Way and not the End?

Sr EM: Because all I have is the present. Now it might be clearer why I define Zen as experiencing fully at all times, at every now.

Q: Where are you going to go when you die?

Sr EM: Sangye has invited me to the visitors' room for a cup of tea when I finish here. I shall go with her. [*Prolonged applause.*]

Q: Does sitting wipe away the dust?

Sr EM: Yes it does. We all carry around quite a bit of garbage, and sitting is the only way I know to get rid of it, at least to lessen the load. Change is of our essence too. I have frequently spoken of Yamada Koun Roshi, and now I'd like to mention his wife, who complemented him in so many ways. She was and still is the mother of us all, and one of her talents is mimicry. Having observed us all from the time we first went to see the *Roshi*, she has keenly in her memory the different stages we went through. A rehearsal of our prematurity is part of every celebrating party.

Q: Can you put it all in a nutshell?

Sr EM: When I'm hungry, I eat.
When I'm tired I sleep.
It's been a long day,
So I'll finish and say:
Good night.

The Oxford Zen Centre of the Sanbo Kyodan has adopted and adapted several chants for its use, two of which are presented here.

(1) Before *teisho*:

Leader The wisdom of God says this:
Sangha Source of all being,
You created me when your purpose first unfolded.
From the oldest of your works,
From everlasting I was firmly set,
From the beginning, before the earth came into being.
The deep was not when I was born.
There were no springs to gush with water.
Before the mountains were settled,
Before the hills I came to birth.
Before you made the earth, the countryside
Or the first grains of the world's dust.
When you fixed the heavens firm, I was there,
When you drew a ring on the surface of the deep.
When you thickened the clouds above,
When you fixed fast the springs of the deep,
When you assigned the seas its boundaries
And the waters will not invade the shore.

When you laid down the foundations of the earth
I was by your side, a master craftsman,
Delighting you day after day,
Ever at play in your presence
At play everywhere in your world
Delighting to be with the children of the earth.

(2) After *teisho*:

Leader   Hakuin Zenji's Song of *Zazen*
Sangha   All beings by nature are Buddha
As ice by nature is water;
Apart from water there is no ice
Apart from beings no Buddha.

How sad that people ignore the near
And search for truth afar
Like those in the midst of water
Crying out for thirst,
Like the child of a wealthy home
Wandering amongst the poor.

The karma of our transmigration
Is our dark path of ignorance;
From dark path to dark path we wander.
When shall we be free from birth and death?

O the *Zenjo* of the Mahayana
To this the highest praise;
Nembutsu, confession, discipline
The many virtues all rise within *zenjo*.

Those who try *zazen* but once
Sweep all their ancient vice away:
Where can evil intentions be?
The Pure Land itself is right here.

Those who hear this truth but once
And listen to it with a grateful heart
Exalting it, revering it,
Gain blessings without end.

Still more, those who turn within
And prove their own self-nature,
Self-nature that is no-nature,
Go far beyond mere cleverness.

They know effect and cause are one,
Not two, not three, the paths run straight
With form that is no form
Going and coming never astray
With thought that is no thought.
Their song and dance are the voice of the law.

Broad is the sky of *samadhi* set free,
Transparent the moonlight of wisdom.
And what more indeed can we seek?
Here is Nirvana itself revealed.
This very place is the Lotus Land,
This very body, the Buddha.

Glossary of Japanese
and Sanskrit Words Used

ango	period of quiet retreat
aikido	art of self-defence by meeting the spirit of the other
batsu	rewarding stick
bompu Zen	ordinary Zen
chonan	eldest son
daijo	great vehicle Zen
Denkoroku	*Rinzai* book of *koans*
dhyana	(Sanskrit) meditation
dojo	place of practice
dokusan	private interview
gassho	gesture of joining hands before the face
gedo Zen	outside-the-way Zen
Hekiganroku	*Rinzai* book of koans
hibachi	deep brazier
Hinayana	small vehicle Buddhism
hobo	disciplinary stick
ikebana	flower arrangement

joriki	settling power
judo	art of self-defence
kado	art of flower arrangement
kaikan	auditorium
kendo	art of fencing
kensho godo	the Way of enlightenment
kinhin	walking meditation
koan	a conundrum which the intellect cannot solve
kokoro	the heart-mind or consciousness
koto	Japanese harp
kyosaku	stick for massaging back and shoulder muscles
Kyosho	Sanbo Kyodan bi-monthly magazine
kyudo	the art of Archery
Mahayana	the large vehicle Buddhism
makyo	surfacing of inner residue on the surface of the mind
michi	the Way
mondo	questions and answers, Zen repartee
Mumonkan	perhaps the most famous collection of *koans*
mudra	hand position during practice
rohatsu	Zen retreat prior to December 8
rosan	12-year period of severe discipline in *Tendai* Buddhism
roshi	honorary title, sometimes given to a Zen master
sado	the art of tea
saijojo	Zen of the highest vehicle in Buddhism
sakura	cherry blossom

samadhi	(Sanskrit) deeper than the ordinary state of consciouness
sangha	community of disciples
sannyasi	holy wanderer
satori	enlightenment
sesshin	Zen retreat
Shakado	Tendai temple on Mount Hiei
shikantaza	just sitting
Shinmeikutsu	Jesuit *zendo* west of Tokyo
shodo	art of Calligraphy
shojo	3rd type of Zen, small vehicle
shoken	first interview with teacher
Shoyoroku	Soto book of *koans*
Tathagata	pure coming and going, Absolute appearance
teisho	a Zen talk
Theravada	Way of the Elders
wasan	song of *zazen*
zabuton	large flat cushion for sitting
zafu	round high cushion for sitting
zammai	deeper than ordinary state of consciousness
zazen	sitting meditation

Acknowledgements and Sources

I wish to thank the Trustees of the Prison Phoenix for their encouragement and offering of time to enlarge the manuscript and prepare it for publication; and in a particular way to the Trust's staff, Sandy Chubb, Colleen Clyne and Nick Daisley for reading the manuscript carefully and offering apt suggestions.

Although they remain in my heart, I cannot begin to name everyone who helped in the various needs of assembling a book, but I do want to mention my gratitude to Hugo Brunner for his fatherly advice and generous backing; Ruben Habito who continues to be only a phone-call away with needed information and affirmation; Giles Semper and Rosamund Webber who have become more than just editor and assistant at HarperCollins.

And as I look out at the late autumnal colours still proclaiming and substantiating all I have tried to say in this book, I acknowledge with a full and grateful heart the myriad conveyers of wisdom in our beautiful world today.

The author and publishers wish to thank the Theosophical Society of the Philippines for releasing the material *Teaching Zen to Christians* ((1993, Manila).

The author and publishers acknowledge with thanks

permission to reproduce copyright material. Where available, copyright information is listed below:

1) Robert Kennedy SJ, *The Challenge of Being an Honest Broker of Both Traditions*, from a talk given at a symposium in 1994 at Lassalle Haus, Switzerland.

2) Hugo Enomiya-Lassalle SJ, *Living in the New Consciousness* (1988, Shambala Publications, Boston).

3) Yamada Koun Roshi, *The Gateless Gate*, (1979, Zen Centre Publications, Los Angeles).

4) Pierre Teilhard de Chardin SJ, *The Hymn of the Universe*, Pensée 17 (© in the original French, 1961 Editions du Seuil, Paris; © in the English translation, 1965 HarperCollins*Publishers*).

5) Dom Wulstan Mork OSB, *The Biblical Meaning of Man* (1967, Bruce Publishing Company, Milwaukee).

6) John of the Cross, *Spiritual Canticle*, stanza 39, translation from the private notes of Hugo Enomiya-Lassalle SJ.

7) John Daishin Buksbazen, *To Forget the Self* (1977, Zen Centre Publications, Los Angeles).

8) Paul de Jaegher SJ, *One with Jesus* (1929, Burns & Oates).

9) Federation of Asian Bishops' Conferences, *Prayer – the Life of the Church in Asia*, (1979, Cardinal Bea Institute, Manila).

10) Yasutani Hakuun Roshi, *Zen no Shinzui: Mumonkan* (1973, Shunjusha, Tokyo).

11) John of the Cross, *The Ascent of Mount Carmel Book 3*, extracts from chapters 6 & 7, translation from the private notes of Hugo Enomiya-Lassalle SJ.

12) *see* note 3.

13) Abhishiktananda, *Prayer* (SPCK, London, ISPCK, Delhi and the Westminster John Knox Press, Kentucky).

14) Jostein Gaarder, *Sophie's World* (1995, Phoenix House).

15) *see* note 8.

16) *see* note 8.

The Prison Phoenix Trust, 1996

'I'm not trying to sell or market anything; all I'm saying is, if you want to turn your life around there is a way to do it.'

Letter from a Prison Phoenix Trust Counsellor

The Prison Phoenix Trust was founded in 1988 to help prisoners to the realization that being in prison gives them a unique opportunity for real change. We encourage them to look beyond just 'doing time', to discover their true inner nature and to take responsibility for their own actions. Basic to this approach is the belief that there is a spiritual being inside all of us, however fearful or lost, and whether we are of any faith or none.

We teach simple meditation techniques, known and practised by all major religions for centuries, to find spiritual awareness, and we give support to prisoners on their own journeys. Ann Wetherall, the Trust's founder, wrote to an inmate, 'All you need for meditation is your body, your mind and your breath. Being shut in your cell for much of the day provides you with an excellent opportunity for change.'

Word about the Prison Phoenix Trust is spread mainly through the prison grapevine: prisoners get in touch with us, and we respond. We are now in contact with people in every prison and young offender unit in Britain. Once a prisoner contacts us, we send them Bo Lozoff's book *We're All Doing Time*, and *Becoming Free through Meditation and Yoga* by Sister Elaine and Sandy Chubb – tape copies exist for those people serving time who cannot read. Prisoners also write to tell us of the astonishing impact these books and their message can have on their lives.

We hold workshops in prisons throughout the UK, and follow these up wherever we can by establishing weekly classes run by qualified local yoga and meditation teachers, to whom we give training on the issues which will confront them in prison. Right now, some sixty teachers are holding classes in prisons around the country.

But does it really work? Teachers, Governors and prison chaplains confirm that the work of the Trust does alter prisoners' behaviour and their outlook on life, and we see it so often in our own correspondence and meetings with those people themselves.

Society needs to be protected from crime, and prison may seem the best way of achieving this. But prison can serve as a school for crime, and a place of fear and brutality which compounds the damage people have already suffered in their lives.

Yet imprisonment can be turned into a positive experience, and this is what we try to achieve. Our small office in Oxford is staffed by people who are trained and very experienced in meditation, yoga and counselling, and we have the support and assistance of many Governors and other Home Office staff.

We are a registered charity; we are not endowed, and depend on donations to continue our work.

The Prison Phoenix Trust, PO Box 328, Oxford OX1 1PJ
(registered charity no. 327907)

Patrons: Mrs Lorna St Aubyn, Rabbi Lionel Blue, Dr Sheila Cassidy, Baroness Lucy Faithfull OBE, Fr Laurence Freeman OSB, Mr Jeremy Irons, His Honour Judge Stephen Tumim.